More Praise for
REENGINEERING THE CORPORATION

"Already, a number of books on the subject [of reengineering] are coming out. . . . But the first one you should spend your time and money on is the work of reengineering originators—Hammer and CSC/Index Chairman James Champy. Indeed, in writing *Reengineering the Corporation*, Hammer and Champy have done some badly needed reengineering of the business book genre. . . . It lays out the reasons reengineering is important, and it provides the how-to information demanded by practicing managers. . . . *Reengineering* may well be the best-written, most well-reasoned business book for the managerial masses since *In Search of Excellence*."

—JOHN BYRNE, *Business Week*

"Michael Hammer and James Champy are the fire-breathing revolutionaries [whose] highly influential, highly readable *Reengineering the Corporation* suggests that we all get busy reexamining every single process and rebuilding U.S. business from the ground up.

—*Fortune*

"There is no better source for getting excited about reengineering."

—*Sloan Management Review*

"*Reengineering the Corporation* is an important book that describes the principles behind a new and systematic approach to structuring and managing work. Written in clear, readable prose, the book describes the what, the why, and the how of business reengineering. Whether they are chief executives, functional executives, or professionals, decision makers need to read this book."

—PETER F. DRUCKER

"Particularly good are the chapters that explore the impact of corporate reinvention on work itself . . . and the enabling role of technology."

—*Inc.* magazine

REENGINEERING
THE CORPORATION

REENGINEERING THE CORPORATION

A MANIFESTO FOR
BUSINESS REVOLUTION

MICHAEL HAMMER
& JAMES CHAMPY

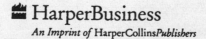
HarperBusiness
An Imprint of HarperCollinsPublishers

HarperCollins books may be purchased for educational, business, or sales promotional use. For information please write: Special Markets Department, HarperCollins Publishers, Inc., 10 East 53rd Street, New York, NY 10022.

Library of Congress Cataloging-in-Publication Data

Hammer, Michael, 1948-
    Reengineering the corporation : a manifesto for business revolution/Michael Hammer and James Champy.
        p. cm.
    Originally published: 1993. With new prologue.
    Includes index.
    ISBN 0-06-662112-7 (pb)
    1. Organizational change. 2. Corporate reorganizations. 3. Reengineering (Management) I. Champy, James, 1942- II. Title.

HD58.8 .H356 2001
658.4'063—dc21

02 03 04 05 ❖/RRD 10 9 8 7 6 5 4 3 2

For my parents, who showed me the path that I follow; for my wife, with whom I travel it; and for my children, whose paths await them.

M. H.

For my wife, Lois, from whom I have learned so much; and for my son, Adam, for whom I have the joy of teaching.

J. C.

ACKNOWLEDGMENTS

The central thesis of this book—that corporations must undertake nothing less than a radical reinvention of how they do their work—may strike some as extreme. But for the risk-averse, we hasten to add that our recommendations and conclusions are based on the successes now being realized by a handful of extraordinary organizations. We owe a great deal to these companies and to their far-sighted executives and managers.

We also owe a debt of gratitude to the many colleagues and teachers from whom we have learned so much over the years. To list them all would be impossible, but two deserve special mention: Peter Drucker and Tony Athos, whose insights into organizations inform all our work. We also want to thank the many individuals as CSC Index who shared with us their consulting experiences, gathered case material, and helped to bring this book to fruition. Their contributions can be found throughout the book.

We particularly wish to thank the individuals who were invaluable in the process of making this book a reality: Donna Sammons Carpenter, Maurice Coyle, and Abby Solomon, whose extraordinary editorial skills helped turn an inchoate mass into a coherent narrative; Helen Rees, our literary agent who taught us the "business" of publishing; and Virginia Smith, Adrian Zackheim, and Erin Richnow, our editors at HarperBusiness who supported our work at every step.

Finally, our greatest appreciation is reserved for all those people currently helping to make reengineering a reality in their own organizations and advancing our collective understanding of this new age in business.

CONTENTS

PROLOGUE:
REENGINEERING FOR THE
TWENTY-FIRST CENTURY

Reengineering is back.

Conventional wisdom suggests that reengineering was a management fad of the early 1990s, one that like all such fads had its short time in the sun and then deservedly passed into obscurity. Today, one can scarcely pick up a self-styled guide to the "new economy" without encountering dismissive comments about reengineering as quintessential "old economy" thinking. A kinder version of this story asserts that reengineering was a concept suited to its times: one of recession and retreat, when American companies were running from the Japanese colossus. Costs were out of control, quality was abysmal, and the U.S. economy seemed to be in free fall. It was a time of drastic steps, of takeover artists prowling Wall Street, of slash-and-burn downsizing, of reengineering.

Now, however, we have been saved by Bill Gates, the microprocessor, and the Internet. Information technology has driven U.S. productivity through the roof, while a combination of economic mismanagement and social inflexibility has obstructed our competitors. Reengineering may have been relevant once upon a time, but that time is long gone. An even harsher version of this story paints reengineering either as an outright fraud—empty slogans without any substance—or nothing more than a synonym for downsizing.

All of this is wrong.

Reengineering is not gone; it is alive and well. In fact, it is a little misleading to say that reengineering is back. The truth is, it never went away. Out of the glare of the spotlight, real businesses have been using reengineering assiduously to transform vast segments of their operations. Order filling, manufacturing, purchasing, and customer service are some of the major areas that today bear no resemblance to how they were performed just a few years ago. Reengineering gave birth to such notions as assigning a single person to perform all the steps involved in handling a customer service request; having order fulfillment performed by a colocated, cross-functional team; building products in response to actual customer orders rather than to forecasts of demand; having low-cost items procured by the people who need them rather than by the company's purchasing department; and many others.

Reengineering is, in fact, one of the success stories of business history. Once considered revolutionary, these practices are now commonplace, and they have played a major role in the resurgence of U.S. companies. IBM, profiled in Chapter 11, is just one of the many giants saved from decline or even extinction by a concerted program of reengineering. American Express, American Standard, Ford, Chrysler, Texas Instruments, and Duke Power are but a few of the *Fortune* 500 that succeeded at reengineering their businesses.

Indeed, the impact of reengineering has been felt not only at the individual level but at the macroeconomic level as well. To attribute the current strength of the U.S. economy solely to reengineering would be excessive. Still, it joins other significant factors, such as sound monetary policy and an interesting surge of entrepreneurial spirit, as one of the key drivers.

Were it not for reengineering, many sectors of the U.S. economy would not be flourishing as they are now. Prices would still be too high, quality would still be too low, and customers would still be looking offshore. American companies would have been unable to respond to the great changes in customer demand, and the threats posed by foreign competitors and aggressive start-ups.

The most striking feature of the contemporary U.S. economy is that neither prices nor wages are rising, despite high demand and low unemployment. In other words, the monster of inflation has been pushed back into its cage. It is correct, but insufficient, to ascribe this miracle to the Federal Reserve's steady hand or to companies' inability to raise prices. If companies today were still operating as they were fifteen years ago, these conditions could not remain stable. If costs are out of control and you cannot raise prices, you go out of business. If your customers' demand for your product increases your own demand for labor, then wages will rise. Because companies have been reengineering, they can maintain profit margins in the face of declining prices and avoid increasing their workforces when confronted with escalating demand.

It is particularly ironic that information technology has been proclaimed as the force behind the renaissance of U.S. industry; in fact, reengineering has been the key that unlocked the potential of this technology. Merely overlaying new technology on old ways of doing business achieves very little. As one wag put it, "IT allows us to make worse decisions sooner." Indeed, until the advent of reengineering, companies were hard-pressed to identify major performance benefits from many of their systems investments. Reengineering showed companies how to transform their processes and ways of working to capitalize on technology.

Why, then, is reengineering held in such ill repute in some circles? We leave the definitive account of this phenomenon to some future business or social historian. Our view is that what occurred was an inevitable backlash to the excessive enthusiasm with which the press and business public first embraced reengineering. In the early 1990s, there was scarcely a business magazine that did not run a cover story on reengineering, and, likewise, there was scarcely a corporation that did not start a reengineering effort. More than a touch of hysteria permeated this phenomenon. Through the 1980s, U.S. companies had been searching desperately, and in vain, for some way to permanently improve their operations. Everything they tried either did not work or produced positive results only fleetingly.

Then reengineering, which already had a successful track record, became more widespread. The experiences of Ford, Kodak, Union Carbide, and the numerous other companies cited in this book, in our other publications, and in the early press reports, made it clear that reengineering was not a hypothesis: It actually *worked*.

Perhaps predictably, reengineering quickly became a bandwagon that everyone tried to jump on; but, problematically, not everyone knew precisely what it was he or she was getting involved in. "Give me reengineering, whatever it is, and give it to me fast," was the command from many uniformed chief executives. This was a situation ripe for disaster. Reengineering came to be viewed as an easy panacea that the CEO can simply delegate. And these are erroneous conclusions. Many managers did not want to read the book, consider seriously what the term meant, or make difficult and significant choices. Instead, they looked for simple ways to reengineer and found a plethora of equally uninformed consultants who were eager to help.

Soon "reengineering" became devoid of meaning. Some companies used it as a generic term for change or as a synonym for whatever activities they had underway that fell under the umbrella of improvement, from rebuilding their information systems to changing their human resource strategy. Yet these same companies maintained extravagant expectations of their "reengineering" efforts, and when these were not met, they naturally attributed this failure to the concept itself. The press, at first wildly enthusiastic about these ideas, now seized upon the "failures" and proclaimed the age of reengineering at an end. But despite this hue and cry, the companies that were accurately and skillfully implementing reengineering were harvesting spectacular benefits.

Reengineering has, in fact, been an enormous success. Nonetheless, it has not yet realized its full potential. On the one hand, it is just now getting underway in some industries (banking and utilities, for example) that had been able until now to avoid making fundamental operating changes. Moreover, even companies that have been working with the ideas for some time have not completed their efforts. On the other hand, new technology is creating opportunities for an entirely new wave of reengineering efforts. In the 1990s, reengineering was implemented in the back office, the factory, and the warehouse. For the new century, it is being applied to the front office and the revenue-producing side of the business: product development, sales, and marketing.

From its inception, reengineering has been a close partner of information technology. Technology enables the processes that are the essence of reengineering to be redesigned. The two have a symbiotic relationship: Without reengineering, information technology delivers little payoff; without information technology, little reengineering can be done. The most important reengineering-related technology of the last five years has been enterprise resource planning (ERP), an integrated software system that supports not individual functional areas but complete business processes. Companies that have attempted to implement an ERP system without first (or simultaneously) reengineering their processes were disappointed by the modest payoffs they received (outside the narrow domain of improved information technology operations and cost). On the other hand, those companies that linked the two—such as IBM, Owens Corning, Amoco, and General Mills—achieved prodigious payoffs. The next wave of reengineering will be closely linked with a technology that integrates not just corporate functions but entire corporations.

As everyone who has not been in hibernation for years knows, we are living in the age of the Internet. It is hard to recall any other innovation that has received as much press or as much hype. Yet businesses will only be able to harness the true power of the Internet if they realize that it too must be tied to reengineering. The genesis of reengineering lies in a phrase one of us coined in the late 1980s: "Automating a mess yields an automated mess." Unless an organization reconceptualized its operations, overlaying new technology on these operations accomplished little.

Today, that slogan has been updated: "Putting a Web site in front of lousy business processes merely advertises how lousy they are." In the absence of robust, reengineered processes, electronic commerce is a nightmare, not a dream. Nonreengineered processes for handling and filling orders are so complex and unreliable that they can barely be performed by trained specialists; to inflict them on an unmediated basis on innocent customers is positively cruel. Selling over the Internet demands a fresh round of reengineering, even for those companies that have just completed their last round.

IBM, for instance, reengineered most of its processes in the mid-1990s, but has just embarked on it again, this time to "Web-enable" these same processes for electronic commerce. *Business Week* recognized the relationship between the Internet and reengineering in its first special report on electronic business: It dubbed the implementation of e-commerce "e-engineering." The Internet demands new ways of working, and reengineering is the tool that can create them.

The hallmark of first-wave reengineering is that it dissolved functional boundaries in order to concentrate on the end-to-end business processes that create all real customer value and transcend these boundaries. The new wave of Internet-enabled reengineering is breaking down the walls that separate corporations from each other. Processes do not stop at corporate doorsteps. Product development, planning and forecasting, and a host of other processes are really interenterprise in nature; they entail work by both customer and supplier. The Internet facilitates the reengineering of these intercorporate processes by allowing information to be shared across corporate boundaries.

In short, the reengineering agenda is far from complete. More and more companies are revving their reengineering engines to reinvent how they work with their customers and suppliers. It is to help them get grounded in the basic principles of reengineering that we have updated and reissued this book.

When our publisher approached us about issuing a new edition, we quietly groaned. It had been some time since we last read this book, and we assumed that if it was going to be relevant to a new generation of reengineers, it would have to be completely rewritten. With some surprise and substantial pleasure, we realized that what we wrote in 1992 remains valid in the new millennium. Certainly, the basic motivations for reengineering—the three Cs of customers, competition, and change that we explore in Chapter 1—are as germane now as ever. The concept of process is as applicable in the front office and across corporate boundaries as it was in the back room. The techniques of process design and the roles of process owner, leader, and design team still work. On the whole, we have made only minor editorial changes to maintain the book's accuracy and relevance.

We have, however, prepared an entirely new set of case studies for this edition (Chapters 10 through 12). The original version of the book described the experiences of the early pioneers. While their stories were important and instructive, in many cases, the companies that followed and learned from them have surpassed those trailblazers. Our new case studies focus on three well-known companies—Duke Power, IBM, and Deere. Their leadership positions at the end of the 1990s are due in no small part to the success of their reengineering programs.

We welcome to this new edition old friends and new acquaintances alike. Those already knowledgeable on the subject of reengineering will learn much from the new case studies. Those new to the topic have the opportunity to begin with the basics and, as the book continues, become acquainted with the most current thinking in this area.

We hope that this book will be as useful for the new wave of reengineering as it was for the first one. Reengineering is here to stay. Until the world stops changing, it will remain an essential business tool. We feel confident that this book will have nearly as long a lifetime as its subject matter.

CHAPTER 1

THE CRISIS THAT WILL NOT GO AWAY

Not a company exists whose management doesn't say, at least for public consumption, that it wants an organization flexible enough to adjust quickly to changing market conditions, lean enough to beat any competitor's price, innovative enough to keep its products and services technologically fresh, and dedicated enough to deliver maximum quality and customer service.

So, if managements want companies that are lean, nimble, flexible, responsive, competitive, innovative, efficient, customer-focused, and profitable, why are so many businesses bloated, clumsy, rigid, sluggish, noncompetitive, uncreative, inefficient, disdainful of customer needs, and losing money? The answers lie in how these companies do their work and why they do it that way. The results companies achieve are often very different from the results that their managements desire, as these examples illustrate.

• A manufacturer we visited has, like many other companies, set a goal of filling customer orders quickly, but this goal is proving elusive. Like most companies in its industry, this company uses a multi-tiered distribution system. That is, factories send finished goods to a central distribution center (CDC). The CDC in turn ships the products to regional distribution centers (RDCs), smaller warehouses that receive and fill customer orders. One of the RDCs covers the geographical area in which the CDC is located. In fact, the two occupy the same building. Often and inevitably RDCs do not have the goods they need to fill customers' orders. This particular RDC, however, *should* be able to get missing products quickly from the CDC located across the hall, but it doesn't work out that way. That's because even on a rush/expedite order, the process takes *eleven days:* one day for the RDC to notify the CDC that it needs parts; five days for the CDC to check, pick, and dispatch the order; and five days for the RDC to officially receive and shelve the goods, and then pick and pack the customer's order. One reason the process takes so long is that RDCs are rated by the amount of time they take to respond to customer orders, but CDCs are not. Their performance is judged on other factors: inventory costs, inventory turns, and labor costs. Hurrying to fill an RDC's rush order will hurt the CDC's own performance rating. Consequently, the RDC does not even attempt to obtain rush goods from the CDC located across the hall. Instead, it has them air-shipped overnight from another RDC. The costs? Air freight bills alone run into millions of dollars annually; each RDC has a unit that does nothing but work with other RDCs looking for goods; and the same goods are moved and handled more times than good sense would dictate. The RDCs and the CDC are doing their jobs, but the overall system just doesn't work.

• Often the efficiency of a company's parts comes at the expense of the efficiency of its whole. A plane belonging to a major U. S. airline was grounded one afternoon for repairs at airport A, but the nearest mechanic qualified to perform the repairs worked at airport B. The manager at airport B refused to send the mechanic to airport A that afternoon, because after completing the repairs the mechanic would have had to stay overnight at a hotel and the hotel bill would come out of manager B's budget. Instead, the mechanic was dispatched to airport A early the following morning; this enabled him to fix the plane and return home the same day. A multimillion dollar aircraft sat idle, and the airline lost hundreds of thousands of dollars in revenue, but manager B's budget wasn't hit for a $100 hotel bill. Manager B was neither foolish nor careless. He was doing exactly what he was supposed to be doing: controlling and minimizing his expenses.

• Work that requires the cooperation and coordination of several different departments within a company is often a source of trouble. When retailers return unsold goods for credit to a consumer products manufacturer we know, thirteen separate departments are involved. Receiving accepts the goods, the warehouse returns them to stock, inventory management updates records to reflect their return, promotions determines at what price the goods were actually sold, sales accounting adjusts commissions, general accounting updates the financial records, and so on. Yet no single department or individual is in charge of handling returns. For each of the departments involved, returns are a low-priority distraction. Not surprisingly, mistakes often occur. Returned goods end up "lost" in the warehouse. The company pays sales commissions on *un*sold goods. Worse, retailers do not get the credit that they expect, and they become angry, which effectively undoes all of sales and marketing's efforts. Unhappy retailers are less likely to promote the manufacturer's new products. They also delay paying their bills, and often pay only what *they* think they owe after deducting the value of the returns. This throws the manufacturer's accounts receivable department into turmoil, since the customer's check doesn't match the manufacturer's invoice. Eventually, the manufacturer simply gives up, unable to trace what really happened. Its own estimate of the annual costs and lost revenues from returns and related problems runs to *nine figures*. From time to time, management attempts to tighten up the disjointed returns process, but it no sooner gets some departments working well than new problems crop up in others.

• Even when the work involved could have a major impact on the bottom line, companies often have no one in charge. As part of the government's approval process for a major new drug, for instance, a pharmaceutical company needed field study results on thirty different patients who took the medicine for one week. Obtaining this information took the company *two years*. A company scientist spent four months developing the study and specifying the kind of data to be collected. Actually designing the study took only two weeks, but getting other scientists to review the design took fourteen. Next, a physician spent two months scheduling and conducting interviews in order to recruit other doctors who would identify appropriate patients and actually administer the trial drug. Securing permission from all the hospitals involved took a month, most of which was spent waiting for replies. The physicians administering the one-week dose were paid in advance, so they had no incentive to accelerate their work. Collecting the forms that the doctors filled out took two months. Next, the study administrator sent the forms to data entry, where errors were discovered on about 90 percent of them. Back they went to the protocol designer, who sent them to the study administrator, who returned them to the physicians, who tried to correct the mistakes. As a result of its own field study process (not the government's approval process), the company lost nearly two years' profits, worth millions of dollars, on this drug, as it had on many others. Yet, to this day no one at the company has overall responsibility for getting field studies done.

These are stories taken more or less at random from our experiences; they could be replicated endlessly. These companies are not exceptions; they are the rule. This is not how corporate executives say they want their companies to behave, yet this behavior persists nonetheless. Why?

Corporations do not perform badly because, as some critics have claimed, workers are lazy and managements are inept. Our record of industrial and technological accomplishment in the last century is proof enough that managements are not inept and workers do work. Ironically, the explanation for why companies perform badly is the identical explanation for why they used to perform so well.

During the twentieth century, American entrepreneurs led the world in creating business organizations that set the pace for product development, production, and distribution. No wonder these companies served as organizational models for businesses around the globe. American corporations delivered affordable factory-made goods, built and operated railroads that spanned the continent, created technological advances, such as the telephone and automobile, that changed the way we lived, and produced the highest standard of living the world had ever known. That these same companies and their descendants no longer perform well isn't because of some intrinsic flaw; it is because the world in which they operate has changed beyond the limits of their capacity to adjust or evolve. The principles on which they are organized were superbly suited to the conditions of an earlier era, but they can stretch only so far.

Advanced technologies, the disappearance of boundaries between national markets, and the altered expectations of customers who now have more choices than ever before have combined to make the goals, methods, and basic organizing principles of the classical corporation sadly obsolete. Renewing their competitive capabilities isn't an issue of getting the people in these companies to work harder, but of learning to work differently. This means that companies and their employees must unlearn many of the principles and techniques that brought them success for so long.

Most companies today—no matter what business they are in, how technologically sophisticated their product or service, or where their business is located—can trace their work styles and organizational roots back to the prototypical pin factory that Adam Smith described in *The Wealth of Nations*, published in 1776. Smith, a philosopher and economist, recognized that the technology of the industrial revolution had created unprecedented opportunities for manufacturers to increase worker productivity and thus reduce the cost of goods, not by small percentages, which one might achieve by persuading an artisan to work a little faster, but by orders of magnitude. In *The Wealth of Nations,* Smith, a radical thinker and forebear of the business consultant, explained what he called the principle of the division of labor.

Smith's principle embodied his observations that some number of specialized workers, each performing a single step in the manufacture of a pin, could make far more pins in a day than the same number of generalists, each engaged in making whole pins. "One man," Smith wrote, "draws out the wire, another straightens it, a third cuts it, a fourth points it, a fifth grinds it at the top for receiving the head; to make the head requires two or three distinct operations; to put it on is a peculiar business, to whiten the pins is another; it is even a trade by itself to put them into the paper." Smith reported that he had visited a small factory, employing only ten people, each of whom was doing just one or two of the eighteen specialized tasks involved in making a pin. "These ten persons could make among them upwards of forty-eight thousand pins in a day. But if they had all wrought separately and independently, and without any of them having been educated to this peculiar business, they certainly could not each of them have made twenty, perhaps not one pin in a day."

The division of labor increased the productivity of pin makers by a factor of hundreds. The advantage, Smith wrote, "is owing to three different circumstances; first, to the increase of dexterity in every particular workman; secondly, to the saving of the time which is commonly lost in passing from one species of work to another; and lastly, to the invention of a great number of machines which facilitate and abridge labor, and enable one man to do the work of many."

Today's airlines, steel mills, accounting firms, and computer chip makers have all been built around Smith's central idea—the division or specialization of labor and the consequent fragmentation of work. The larger the organization, the more specialized is the worker and the more separate steps into which the work is fragmented. This rule applies not only to manufacturing jobs. Insurance companies, for instance, typically assign separate clerks to process each line of a standardized form. A clerk completes his or her task and then passes the form to another clerk, who processes the next line. These workers never complete a job; they just perform piecemeal tasks.

Over time, U.S. companies became the best in the world at translating Smith's organizing principles into working business organizations, even though, when Smith first published his ideas in 1776, not much of a domestic market existed for American-made goods. Americans, who numbered only 3.9 million, were separated from one another by bad roads and poor communications. Philadelphia, with 45,000 residents, was the fledgling nation's largest city.

Over the next half century, though, the population exploded and the domestic market expanded accordingly. The population of Philadelphia, for example, quadrupled, though New York was now the largest city with 313,000 people. Manufacturing facilities sprouted around the country.

Part of this growth occurred because of innovative changes in the ways in which goods could be shipped. In the 1820s, Americans began building railroads, which not only extended and accelerated economic development but also moved the evolution of business management technology forward. It was railroad companies that invented the modern business bureaucracy—a significant innovation then and an essential one if industrial organizations were going to grow beyond the span of one person's control.

To prevent collisions on single-track lines that carried trains in both directions, railroad companies invented formalized operating procedures and the organizational structure and mechanisms required to carry them out. Management created a rule for every contingency they could imagine, and lines of authority and reporting were clearly drawn. The railroad companies literally programmed their workers to act only in accordance with the rules, which was the only way management knew to make their one-track systems predictable, workable, and safe. Programming people to conform to established procedures remains the essence of bureaucracy even now. The command-and-control systems in place in most companies today embody the same principles the railroads introduced 150 years ago.

The next large evolutionary steps in the development of today's business organization came early in the twentieth century from two automobile pioneers: Henry Ford and Alfred Sloan.

Ford improved on Smith's concept of dividing work into tiny, repeatable tasks. Instead of having skilled assemblers build entire cars from parts they would fit together, Ford reduced each worker's job to installing a single part in a prescribed manner. Initially, workers walked from one assembly stand to the next, taking themselves to the work. The moving assembly line, the innovation for which Ford is best remembered, simply brought the work to the worker.

In breaking down car assembly into a series of uncomplicated tasks, Ford made the jobs themselves infinitely simpler, but he made the process of coordinating the people performing those jobs and of combining the results of their tasks into a whole car far more complex.

Then Alfred Sloan stepped in. Sloan, the successor to General Motors' founder William Durant, created the prototype of the management system that Ford's immensely more efficient factory system demanded.

Neither Henry Ford nor Durant ever learned how to manage the huge, sprawling organizations that their success with assembly-line production both necessitated and made possible—the engineering, manufacturing, assembly, and marketing operations. Durant, especially, with GM's far greater mix of cars and models, was constantly finding that the company had produced too many of one model for current market conditions or that production had to be suspended because not enough raw materials had been procured. After Sloan took over at GM, he made the system Ford had pioneered complete, and it is this total system to which the term "mass production" applies today.

Sloan created smaller, decentralized divisions that managers could oversee from a small corporate headquarters simply by monitoring production and financial numbers. Sloan set up one division for each car model—Chevrolet, Pontiac, Buick, Oldsmobile, and Cadillac—plus others making components such as generators (Delco) and steering gears (Saginaw).

Sloan was applying Adam Smith's principle of the division of labor to management just as Ford had applied it to production. In Sloan's view, corporate executives did not need specific expertise in engineering or manufacturing; specialists could oversee those functional areas. Instead, executives needed financial expertise. They had only to look at "the numbers"—sales, profit and loss, inventory levels, market share, and so forth—generated by the company's various divisions to see if those divisions were performing well; if not, they could demand appropriate corrective action.

Sloan's management innovations saved General Motors from early oblivion and, what's more, also solved the problems that had kept other companies from expanding. The new marketing specialists and financial managers that Sloan's system required complemented the company's engineering professionals. The head of GM firmly established the division of professional labor in parallel with the division of manual labor that had already taken place on the factory floor.

The final evolutionary step in the development of corporations as we know them today came about in the United States between the end of World War II and the 1960s, a period of enormous economic expansion. The regimes of Robert McNamara at Ford, Harold Geneen at ITT, and Reginald Jones at General Electric epitomized management of that era. Through elaborate planning exercises, senior managers determined the businesses in which they wanted to be, how much capital they should allocate to each, and what returns they would expect the operating managers of these businesses to deliver to the company. Large staffs of corporate controllers, planners, and auditors acted as the executives' eyes and ears, ferreting out data about divisional performance and intervening to adjust the plans and activities of operating managers.

The organizational model developed in the United States spread rapidly into Europe and then to Japan after World War II. Designed for a period of heavy demand and accelerating growth, this form of corporate organization suited the circumstances of the postwar times perfectly.

An unrelenting demand for goods and services, at home and abroad, shaped the economic environment of the time. Deprived of material goods, first by the Depression, then by the war, customers were more than happy to buy whatever companies offered them. Rarely did they demand high quality and service. Any house, any car, any refrigerator was infinitely better than none at all.

In the 1950s and 1960s, the chief operational concern of company executives was capacity—that is, being able to keep up with ever-increasing demand. If a company built too much productive capacity too soon, it could go deep in the red financing its new plants. But if it built too little capacity, or built it too late, the company could lose market share from its inability to produce. To solve these problems, companies developed ever more complex systems for budgeting, planning, and control.

The standard, pyramidal organizational structure of most organizations was well suited to a high-growth environment because it was scalable. When a company needed to grow, it could simply add workers as needed at the bottom of the chart and then fill in the management layers above.

This kind of organizational structure was also ideally suited for control and planning. By breaking work down into pieces, supervisors could ensure consistent and accurate worker performance, and the supervisors' supervisors could do the same. Budgets were easily approved and monitored department by department, and plans were generated and pursued on the same basis.

This organizational form also made for short training periods, since few production tasks were complicated or difficult. Moreover, as new office technology became available in the 1960s, companies were encouraged to break down even more of their white-collar work into small, repeatable tasks, which could also be mechanized or automated.

As the number of tasks grew, however, the overall processes of producing a product or delivering a service inevitably became increasingly complicated, and managing such process became more difficult. The growing number of people in the middle of the corporate organization chart—the functional or middle managers—was one of the prices companies paid for the benefits of fragmenting their work into simple, repetitive steps and organizing themselves hierarchically.

Another disadvantage was the increasing distance between senior management and users of their product or service. How customers were responding to the company's strategy was measured only in numbers, never in faces.

These, then, are the roots of today's corporation, the principles, forged by necessity, on which today's companies have structured themselves. If modern companies thin-slice work into meaningless tasks, it is because that is how efficiency was once achieved. If they diffuse power and responsibility through massive bureaucracies, it is because that was the way they learned to control sprawling enterprises. If they resist suggestions that they change the way they operate, it is because these organizing principles and the structures to which they gave birth have worked well for decades.

The reality that organizations have to confront, however, is that the old ways of doing business—the division of labor around which companies have been organized since Adam Smith first articulated the principle—simply don't work anymore. Suddenly, the world is a different place. Our here-and-now crisis of competitiveness is not the result of a temporary economic downturn or a low point in the business cycle. Indeed, we can no longer even count on a predictable business cycle—prosperity, followed by recession, followed by renewed prosperity—as we once did. In today's environment, nothing is constant or predictable—not market growth, customer demand, product life cycles, the rate of technological change, or the nature of competition. Adam Smith's world and its way of doing business are yesterday's paradigm.

Three forces, separately and in combination, are driving today's companies deeper and deeper into territory that most of their executives and managers find frighteningly unfamiliar. We call these forces the three Cs: customers, competition, and change. Their names are hardly new, but the characteristics of the three Cs are remarkably different from what they were in the past.

Let's look at the three Cs and how they have changed, beginning with customers.

• Customers take charge

Since the early 1980s, in the United States and other developed countries, the dominant force in the seller-customer relationship has shifted. Sellers no longer have the upper hand; customers do. Customers now tell suppliers what they want, when they want it, how they want it, and what they will pay. This new situation is unsettling to companies that have known life only in the mass market.

In reality, a mass market never existed, but for most of the twentieth century the *idea* of the mass market provided manufacturers and service providers—from Henry Ford's car company to Thomas Watson's computer company—with the useful fiction that their customers were more or less alike. If that was true, or if buyers behaved as if it were true, then companies could assume that a standard product or service—a black car or a big blue computer—would satisfy most of them. Even those who weren't satisfied would buy what was offered, because they had little choice. Mass market suppliers in the United States had relatively few competitors, and most of them offered very similar products and services. In fact, most consumers weren't dissatisfied. They didn't know that anything better or different was available.

Now that they have choices, though, customers no longer behave as if they are all cast in the same mold. Customers—consumers and corporations alike—demand products and services designed for their unique and particular needs. There is no longer any such notion as *the* customer; there is only *this* customer, the one with whom a seller is dealing at the moment and who now has the capacity to indulge his or her own personal tastes. The mass market has broken into pieces, some as small as a single customer.

Individual customers—whether consumers or industrial firms—demand that they be treated individually. They expect products that are configured to their needs, delivery schedules that match their manufacturing plans or work hours, and payment terms that are convenient for them. Individually and in combination, a number of factors have contributed to shifting the balance of market power from producer to consumer.

Consumer expectations soared in the United States when competitors—many of them Japanese—burst upon the market with lower prices combined with higher-quality goods. Then the Japanese introduced new products that established American producers had not had time to bring to market—or maybe hadn't even thought of yet. What's more, the Japanese did it all with levels of service that traditional companies could not match. This was mass production *plus*—plus quality, price, selection, and service.

In the service sector, consumers expect and demand more because they know they can *get* more. Technology, in the form of sophisticated, easily accessible databases, allows service providers and retailers of all kinds to track not only basic information about their customers but their preferences and requirements, thereby laying a new foundation for competitiveness.

In Houston, if a customer calls Pizza Hut to order a pepperoni and mushroom pie, the same kind of pizza that the customer ordered last week, the clerk asks if the caller would like to try a new combination. If the person says yes, the clerk mails him or her discount coupons with offerings customized to that individual's tastes. When a consumer calls Whirlpool's service line, the call is automatically routed to the same service representative the consumer spoke to last time, creating a sense of personal relationship and intimacy in a world of 800 numbers. Mail-order retailers, which have the capability of collecting enormous amounts of data about their customers, have perfected an even higher targeted level of service. Once customers experience this superior service, they do not happily settle for less.

The incredible consolidation of customers in some markets—the growth of megadealers in the automobile business, the handful of fast-food franchises replacing thousands of independent eateries, and the mall-sized discounters that have emptied Main Street storefronts—has also profoundly changed the terms of the seller-customer relationship. If the sign out front now reads "Joe Smith's Oldsmobile, Nissan, Isuzu, Mercedes, Jeep, Honda, and Saturn," then Joe Smith, not General Motors, has the upper hand in negotiations. With so many other brands available to him, Joe needs General Motors less than GM needs him.

The threat of backward integration has also helped to shift power from producers to consumers. Often, customers can now do for themselves what suppliers used to do for them. Companies may not want to, but they can buy the same machines and hire the same people as their vendors. "Do it my way," they can say, "or I will do it myself." Inexpensive and easy-to-learn desktop publishing technology, for instance, gives companies the choice of doing for themselves jobs for which they used to rely on printers.

What holds true for industrial customers also holds true for consumers. When individual depositors realized that they could themselves purchase the same high-grade, short-term government securities and commercial paper that the banks were buying with their deposit money, many of them reduced their balances in those low-interest-bearing accounts, depriving the banks of an important source of revenue.

Customers have gained the upper hand in their relationships with sellers, in part, because customers now have easy access to enormously more data. The information-rich world is made possible by new communications technologies. Anyone can, for instance, log onto the Internet or pick up a daily newspaper and compare rates on CDs from banks all around the country. People now know positively if their local bank is offering a good deal and, if not, who is. An auto dealer today has to assume that any customer has read the appropriate issue of *Consumer Reports*, compared prices and features on the Internet, and is well aware of what the dealer paid the manufacturer for the car. This makes the negotiation process decidedly trickier for the dealer.

For companies that grew up with a mass market mentality, the hardest new reality to accept about customers is that *each one counts.* Lose a customer today and another doesn't just appear. For thirty years after World War II, consumer goods were in chronically short supply. Manufacturers could not produce enough of them at prices sufficiently low to satisfy every possible buyer. The effect of insatiable demand was to give producers the advantage over buyers. In a mass market, to paraphrase the movie *Field of Dreams,* if you build it they will buy.

Consumer goods shortages no longer exist. On the supply side of the equation, more producers now operate around the world. On the demand side, developed countries now have lower population growths. Also, many product markets have matured. Almost everyone who wants one now owns a refrigerator, a videocassette recorder, and a personal computer. Those industries are in a replacement mode. Consequently, consumers wield a great deal of power. They can, in other words, be very choosy.

In short, in place of the expanding mass markets of the past, companies today have customers—business customers and individual consumers—who know what they want, what they want to pay for it, and how to get it on the terms they demand. Customers such as these don't need to deal with companies that don't understand and appreciate this startling change in the customer-buyer relationship.

• Competition intensifies

The second C is competition. It used to be so simple: The company that could get to market with an acceptable product or service at the best price would get a sale. Now, not only does more competition exist, but there are many different kinds.

Niche competitors have changed the face of practically every market. Similar goods sell in different markets on entirely disparate competitive bases: in one market on the basis of price, in another on selection, somewhere else on quality, and elsewhere on service before, during, or after the sale. With trade barriers falling, no company's national turf is protected from overseas competition. When the Japanese—or Germans, French, Koreans, Taiwanese, and so forth—are free to compete in the same markets, just one superior performer can raise the competitive threshold for companies around the world. Caterpillar competes with Komatsu, DuPont with Hoechst, Chase Manhattan with Barclay's. Good performers drive out the inferior, because the lowest price, the highest quality, the best service available from any one of them soon becomes the standard for all competitors. Adequate is no longer good enough. If a company can't stand shoulder to shoulder with the world's best in a competitive category, it soon has no place to stand at all.

Start-up companies that carry no organizational baggage and are not constrained by their histories can enter a market with the next product or service generation before existing companies can even recoup their development costs on the last one. Big is no longer impregnable, and every established company today needs to post a lookout for start-ups—those that are brand-new and those that have been around for a while but still operate on their founders' principles. By that definition, Sun Microsystems is still a start-up, and so is Wal-Mart. Sun's workstation innovation changed the course of history for every computer maker in the world. Wal-Mart reinvented retailing.

Start-ups do not play by the rules. They write new rules about how to run a business. Wal-Mart did not create itself in the image of Sears. Unburdened by Sears's past, it conceived new ways of working that produce better results. Sears's apparent assets—lots of stores employing well-trained salespeople, established supplier relationships, smoothly tuned operating and administrative systems—have turned into liabilities in that they cannot produce the results that Wal-Mart has established as the new competitive standards.

Technology changes the nature of competition in ways companies don't expect. In retailing, for instance, it has allowed manufacturers and retailers, such as Procter & Gamble and Wal-Mart, to merge their distribution and inventory systems in ways that are mutually beneficial. In after-sales service, technology allows innovators to devise entirely new service techniques. Otis Elevator Company, for example, has developed an ingenious computer system for managing the Byzantine task of servicing 93,000 elevators and escalators in North America around the clock. Repair technicians arrive at the scene already briefed on the nature of the problem and the particular machine's maintenance history. By innovating with technology in order to streamline the interaction between themselves and their customers, companies such as Otis expand the limits of the possible, thereby raising customer expectations for all the companies in a market.

• Change becomes constant

Change is the third C. We already know that customers and competition have changed, but so, too, has the nature of change itself. Foremost, change has become both pervasive and persistent. It is the norm.

Not long ago, for example, life insurance companies offered only two products: term and whole life. Today, they supply a constantly changing smorgasbord of products, and the competitive pressure on insurance companies to create new products is constantly increasing.

Moreover, the pace of change has accelerated. With globalization of the economy, companies face a greater number of competitors, each one of which may introduce product and service innovations to the market. The rapidity of technological change also promotes innovation. Product life cycles have gone from years to months. Ford produced the Model T for an entire human generation. The life cycle of a computer product introduced today might stretch to two years, but it is more likely six to nine months. A company in the pension business recently developed a service to take advantage of a quirk in the tax laws and interest rates. Its anticipated market life was exactly three months. Coming to this market late by just thirty days would have cut the company's selling time for the service by a third.

The point is that not only have product and service life cycles diminished, but so has the time available to develop new products and introduce them. Today, companies must move fast or they won't be moving at all.

Moreover, they have to be looking in many directions at once. Executives *think* their companies are equipped with effective change-sensing radars, but most of them aren't. Mostly what they detect are the changes they expect. The brand managers at a consumer goods manufacturer we know assiduously tracked consumer attitudes in order to detect shifts that might affect their products. Their surveys kept giving them good news, but market share took a sudden drop. They did more surveys. Customers loved the products, but market share kept tumbling. It turned out the problem was that the company's sloppy order fulfillment process was infuriating its retailers, who responded by cutting its shelf space, but neither the brand managers nor anyone else at the company had a broad enough perspective to detect and deal with this problem.

The changes that will put a company out of business are those that happen outside the light of its current expectations, and that is the source of most change in today's business environment.

The three Cs—customers, competition, and change—have created a new world for business, and it is becoming increasingly apparent that organizations designed to operate in one environment cannot be fixed to work well in another. Companies created to thrive on mass production, stability, and growth can't be fixed to succeed in a world where customers, competition, and change demand flexibility and quick response.

Some people blame corporate problems on factors beyond management control—closed foreign markets, the low cost of capital, and predatory pricing by foreign companies subsidized by their governments. They blame the federal government's mishandling of the economy, its regulations, and its poor husbandry of natural and human resources. They blame unions or poorly educated and unmotivated workers.

But if these reasons accounted for our dilemma, nearly all companies would be in decline. But they aren't. Sears may be losing its market, but Wal-Mart is thriving. GM has trouble making world-class cars in the United States, but Honda doesn't. The insurance industry, as a whole, may be hemorrhaging money, but some companies, such as Progressive Insurance, earn outstanding returns. In almost every industry, under the same rules and with the same players, the successes of a few companies rebut the excuses of the many.

If managers can't decide why their companies are in trouble, neither do they agree on what to do about it. Some people think companies would bounce back if only they had the right products and services for the times. We reject that thinking, because products have limited life spans, and even the best soon become obsolete. It is not products but the processes that create products that bring companies long-term success. Good products don't make winners; winners make good products.

Some people think companies could cure what ails them by changing their corporate strategies. They should sell one division and buy another, change their markets, get into a different business. They should juggle assets or restructure with a leveraged buyout (LBO). But this kind of thinking distracts companies from making basic changes in the real work they actually do. It also bespeaks a profound contempt for the daily operations of business. Companies are not asset portfolios, but people working together to invent, make, sell, and provide service. If they are not succeeding in the businesses that they are in, it is because their people are not inventing, making, selling, and servicing as well as they should. Playing tycoon might be more exciting for senior managers than dirtying their hands in the mundane details of operations, but it is not more important. "God," said the architect Mies van der Rohe, "is in the details." Van der Rohe was speaking of buildings, but his observation applies equally well to running a business.

Some people, including many managers, blame corporate problems on management deficiencies. If companies were only managed differently and better, they would thrive. But none of the management fads of the last thirty years—not management by objectives, diversification, theory Z, zero-based budgeting, value chain analysis, decentralization, quality circles, "excellence," restructuring, portfolio management, management by walking around, matrix management, intrapreneuring, or one-minute managing—has enabled companies to sustain their competitive performance. They have only distracted managers from the real task at hand.

Some people think that automation is the answer to business problems. True, computers can speed work up, and in the past forty years businesses have spent billions of dollars to automate tasks that people once did by hand. Automating does get some jobs done faster. But fundamentally the same jobs are being done, and that means no fundamental improvements in performance.

Our diagnosis of business problems is simple, but the corrective action that it demands is not as easy to implement as the solutions that have already been tried. Our diagnosis goes to the very heart of what a company does. It rests on the premise that a company that is better than others at the meat and potatoes of its business—inventing products and services, manufacturing or providing them, selling them, filling orders, and serving customers—will beat the competition in the marketplace. We believe that, in general, the difference between winning companies and losers is that winning companies know how to do their work better. If companies want to become winners again, they will have to look to how they get their work done. It is as simple and as formidable as that.

To illustrate what we mean when we talk about a company getting its work done, let's look at a common process found in practically every company. Order fulfillment begins when a customer places an order, ends when the goods are delivered, and includes everything in between. Typically, the process involves a dozen or so steps performed by different people in different departments. Someone in customer service receives the order, logs it in, and checks it for completeness and accuracy. Then the order goes to finance, where someone else runs a credit check on the customer. Next, someone in sales operations determines the price to charge. Then the order travels to inventory control, where someone checks to see if the goods are on hand. If not, the order gets routed to production planning, which issues a back order. Eventually, warehouse operations develops a shipment schedule. Traffic determines the shipment method—rail, truck, air, or water—and picks the route and carrier. Product handling picks the products from the warehouse, verifies the accuracy of the order, assembles the pickings, and loads them. Traffic releases the goods to the carrier, which takes responsibility for delivering them to the customer.

This process may be complex, but, when viewed from the perspective of Adam Smith's division of labor principle and Alfred Sloan's principles of management control and accountability, it does have certain advantages. First, companies don't have to hire people with advanced degrees to get it done. Every person involved in the process has specific responsibility for performing one simple task. Second, everyone in the process is accountable through the bureaucratic chain of command.

Companies must accept trade-offs, however, for keeping the tasks simple and maintaining tight control of employee actions. First, because no one in the company oversees the whole process and its result, no *one* person is responsible for it. No one involved in the process can tell a customer where the order is and when it will arrive. Many people are involved in order fulfillment, but it is no single person's job or the job of any *one* functional unit.

Second, the process is error-prone. Errors are inevitable with so many people having to handle and act separately on the same order.

Preaching quality won't help. Even if every person involved in order fulfillment did his or her job perfectly and in exactly the time allotted, the process would still be slow and error-prone. Too many handoffs exist—nine at least, and more if the order is placed on back order. Each handoff entails queues, batches, and wait times.

Furthermore, classical order fulfillment involves no element of customer service at all. Complex processes involving a dozen people working across departmental lines can't be made flexible enough to deal with special requests or to respond to inquiries. No one is empowered to answer a question or solve a problem. Once an order enters the process, it might as well be lost until it emerges at the other end—whenever that might be.

Merely fixing the pieces of the order fulfillment process won't solve the larger problem. Companies that try to improve their performance by working on the pieces of the process miss this point. In fact, trying to fix what's wrong with companies by tinkering with the individual process pieces is the best way we know to *guarantee* continued bad business performance. Yet, in company after company we have seen, management works at fixing the pieces instead of redesigning the processes by which the company's work gets done.

The core message of our book, then, is this: It is no longer necessary or desirable for companies to organize their work around Adam Smith's division of labor. Task-oriented jobs in today's world of customers, competition, and change are obsolete. Instead, companies must organize work around *process*.

This is an assertion as radical and as far-reaching today as Adam Smith's was in his time. Managers who understand and accept this concept of process-based work will help their companies leap ahead. Those who don't will stay behind.

We write about "processes" throughout the rest of this book, but already it should be apparent why a process perspective is so important to any company that would find its way out of the dilemma that currently confounds business. It should already be possible to see why companies can't be fixed but have to be reinvented.

In most companies today, no one is in charge of the processes. In fact, hardly anyone is even aware of them. Does any company have a vice president in charge of order fulfillment, of getting products to customers? Probably not. Who *is* in charge of developing new products? Everyone—R&D, marketing, finance, manufacturing, and so on—is involved, but no one is in charge.

Companies today consist of functional silos, or stovepipes, vertical structures built on narrow pieces of a process. The person checking the customer's credit is part of the credit department, which is probably part of the finance organization. Inventory picking is performed by workers in the warehouse, who may report to the vice president of manufacturing. Shipping, on the other hand, is part of logistics. People involved in a process look *inward* toward their department and *upward* toward their boss, but no one looks *outward* toward the customer. The contemporary performance problems that companies experience are the inevitable consequences of process fragmentation.

Classical business structures that specialize work and fragment processes are self-perpetuating because they stifle innovation and creativity in an organization. If someone in a functional department actually has a new idea—a better way of filling customer orders, for instance—he or she first has to sell it to the boss, who has to sell it to his or her boss, and so on up the corporate hierarchy. For an idea to win acceptance, everyone along the way must say yes, but killing an idea requires only one no. From the point of view of its designers, this built-in innovation damper is not a flaw in the classic structure but a safeguard against change that might introduce unwarranted risk.

The fragmented processes and specialized structures of companies bred for an earlier day also are unresponsive to large changes in the external environment—the market. Existing process design embodies the assumption that conditions will vary only within narrow, predictable limits. By removing management from operations and fracturing those operations among specialized departments, today's organizations ensure that no one will be in a position to recognize significant change or, if he or she should happen to recognize it, to do anything about it.

Today, fragmented organizations display appalling diseconomies of scale, quite the opposite of what Adam Smith envisioned. The diseconomies show up not in direct labor, but in overhead. If, for instance, an organization does 100 units of work an hour, and each of its workers can do 10 units an hour, the company would need 11 people: 10 workers and 1 supervisor. But if demand for the company's output grew tenfold to 1,000 units of work an hour, the company wouldn't need just 10 times the number of workers plus 1 manager for each 10 new workers. It would need something like 196 people: 100 workers, 10 supervisors, 1 manager, 3 assistant managers, 18 people in a human resources organization, 19 people in long-range planning, 22 in audit and control, and 23 in facilitation and expediting.

This diseconomy of scale is not just bureaucratic proliferation and empire-building, although some of that may be at work too. Rather, it is a consequence of what we call the Humpty Dumpty school of organizational management. Companies take a natural process, such as order fulfillment, and break it into lots of little pieces—the individual tasks that people in the functional departments do. Then, the company has to hire all the king's horses and all the king's men to paste the fragmented work back together again. These king's horses and king's men have titles such as auditor, expediter, controller, liaison, supervisor, manager, and vice president. They are simply the glue that holds together the people who do the real work—the credit checkers, the inventory pickers, the package shippers. In many companies, direct labor costs may be down, but overhead costs are up—way up. Most companies today, in other words, are paying more for the glue than for the real work—a recipe for trouble.

Inflexibility, unresponsiveness, the absence of customer focus, an obsession with activity rather than result, bureaucratic paralysis, lack of innovation, high overhead—these are the legacies of past business practices. These characteristics are not new; they have not suddenly appeared. They have been present all along. It is just that until recently, companies didn't have to worry much about them. If costs were high, they could be passed on to customers. If customers were dissatisfied, they had nowhere else to turn. If new products were slow in coming, customers would wait. The important managerial job was to manage growth, and the rest didn't matter. Now that growth has flattened out, the rest matters a great deal.

The problem is that we are doing business in the twenty-first century with companies designed during the nineteenth century to work well in the twentieth.

We need something entirely different.

CHAPTER 2

REENGINEERING: THE PATH TO CHANGE

When someone asks us for a quick definition of business reengineering, we say that it means starting over. It *doesn't* mean tinkering with what already exists or making incremental changes that leave basic structures intact. It isn't about making patchwork fixes—jury-rigging existing systems so that they work better. It does mean abandoning long-established procedures and looking afresh at the work required to create a company's product or service and deliver value to the customer. It means asking this question: "If I were recreating this company today, given what I know and given current technology, what would it look like?" Reengineering a company means tossing aside old systems and starting over. It involves going back to the beginning and inventing a better way of doing work.

This informal definition is fine for conversation, because it gives people an idea of what we mean by business reengineering. But anyone who wants to apply reengineering to a company needs something more.

How does a company reengineer its business processes? Where

does it begin? Who gets involved? Where do the ideas for radical change come from?

We have watched companies use trial and error to answer these questions about radical change. We have served as advisers to companies that have made such changes and we have observed many others. Out of their experiences and our own emerged the concept of business reengineering, which we have developed into a process for reinventing a company. To perform this process, we and the companies with which we have worked have developed a body of techniques. These are not formulas, but tools that companies can use to reinvent the way their work gets done.

Our experiences with these techniques, and those of our clients, are encouraging. Used properly—that is, with intelligence and imagination—they can lead to breathtaking improvements in performance. The balance of this book is about business reengineering and how people can make it succeed in their companies.

Reengineering Formally Defined

Let's begin, then, with a better definition. "Reengineering," properly, is the fundamental rethinking and radical redesign of business processes to achieve dramatic improvements in critical, contemporary measures of performance, such as cost, quality, service, and speed. This definition contains four key words.

KEY WORD: FUNDAMENTAL

The first key word is *fundamental.* In doing reengineering, businesspeople must ask the most basic questions about their companies and how they operate: Why do we do what we do? And why do we do it the way we do? Asking these fundamental questions forces people to look at the tacit rules and assumptions that underlie the way they conduct their businesses. Often, these rules turn out to be obsolete, erroneous, or inappropriate.

Reengineering begins with no assumptions and no givens; in fact, companies that undertake reengineering must guard against the assumptions that most processes already have embedded in them. To ask "How can we perform customer credit checks more efficiently?" assumes that customer credit must be checked. In many instances, the cost of checking may, in fact, exceed the bad-debt losses that checking avoids. Reengineering first determines *what* a company must do, then *how* to do it. Reengineering takes nothing for granted. It ignores what *is* and concentrates on what *should be*.

KEY WORD: RADICAL

The second key word in our definition is *radical,* which is derived from the Latin word *radix,* meaning "root." Radical redesign means getting to the root of things: not making superficial changes or fiddling with what is already in place, but throwing away the old. In reengineering, radical redesign means disregarding all existing structures and procedures and inventing completely new ways of accomplishing work. Reengineering is about business *reinvention*—not business improvement, business enhancement, or business modification.

KEY WORD: DRAMATIC

The third key word is *dramatic.* Reengineering isn't about making marginal or incremental improvements but about achieving quantum leaps in performance. If a company falls 10 percent short of where it should be, if its costs come in 10 percent too high, if its quality is 10 percent too low, if its customer service performance needs a 10 percent boost, that company does *not* need reengineering. More conventional methods, from exhorting the troops to establishing incremental quality programs, can dig a company out of a 10 percent hole. Reengineering should be brought in only when a need exists for heavy blasting. Marginal improvement requires fine-tuning; dramatic improvement demands blowing up the old and replacing it with something new.

From our experience, we have identified three kinds of companies that undertake reengineering. First are companies that find themselves in deep trouble. They have no choice. If a company's costs are an order of magnitude higher than the competition's or than its business model will allow, if its customer service is so abysmal that customers openly rail against it, if its product failure rate is twice, three times, or five times as great as the competition's, if, in other words, it needs order-of-magnitude improvement, that company clearly needs business reengineering. Ford Motor Company in the early 1980s is a case in point.

Second are companies that are not yet in trouble but whose management has the foresight to see trouble coming. Aetna Life & Casualty in the last half of the 1980s is an example. For the time being, financial results may appear satisfactory, but looming in the distance are storm clouds—new competitors, changing customer requirements or characteristics, an altered regulatory or economic environment—that threaten to sweep away the foundations of the company's success. These companies have the vision to begin reengineering in advance of running into adversity.

The third group of companies undertaking reengineering are those that are in peak condition. They have no discernible difficulties, either now or on the horizon, but their managements are ambitious and aggressive. Examples include Hallmark and Wal-Mart. Companies in this third category see reengineering as an opportunity to further their lead over their competitors. By enhancing their performance, they seek to raise the competitive bar even higher and make life even tougher for everyone else. Clearly, reengineering from a position of strength is hard to do. Why rewrite the rules when you're already winning the game? It has been said that the hallmark of the truly successful company is a willingness to abandon what has long been successful. A truly great company is never satisfied with its current performance. A truly great company willingly abandons practices that have long worked well in the hope and expectation of coming up with something better.

We sometimes explain the distinctions among these three kinds of companies this way: Companies in the first category are desperate; they have hit the wall and are lying injured on the ground. Companies in the second category are cruising along at high speed, but see something rushing toward them in their head lamps. Could it be a wall? Companies in the third category are out for a drive on a clear afternoon, with no obstacles in sight. What a splendid time, they decide, to stop and build a wall for the other guys.

KEY WORD: PROCESSES

The fourth key word is *processes.* Although this word is the most important in our definition, it is also the one that gives most corporate managers the greatest difficulty. Most businesspeople are not process-oriented; they are focused on tasks, on jobs, on people, on structures, but not on processes.

We define a business process as a collection of activities that takes one or more kinds of input and creates an output that is of value to the customer. We illustrated a process in Chapter 1 when we talked about order fulfillment, which takes an order as its input and results in the delivery of the ordered goods. In other words, the delivery of the ordered goods to the customer's hands is the value that the process creates.

Under the influence of Adam Smith's notion of breaking work into its simplest tasks and assigning each of these to a specialist, modern companies and their managers focus on the individual tasks in this process—receiving the order form, picking the goods from the warehouse, and so forth—and tend to lose sight of the larger objective, which is to get the goods into the hands of the customer who ordered them. The individual tasks within this process are important, but none of them matters one whit to the customer if the overall process doesn't work—that is, if the process doesn't deliver the goods.

Reengineering in Practice

We will use three examples of reengineering to illustrate how it works and what it can accomplish for companies. In reading these examples, it is helpful to keep in mind the four key words that characterize reengineering—fundamental, radical, dramatic, and process—but especially process. Task-based thinking—the fragmentation of work into its simplest components and their assignment to specialist workers—has influenced the organizational design of companies for the last 200 years. The shift to process-based thinking is already underway, and that shift is illustrated in the radical changes that mainstream companies such as IBM Credit, Ford Motor, and Kodak have made.

IBM Credit

Our first case concerns IBM Credit Corporation, a wholly owned subsidiary of IBM, which, if it were independent, would rank among the *Fortune* 100 service companies. IBM Credit is in the business of financing the computers, software, and services that the IBM Corporation sells. It is a business of which IBM is fond, since financing customers' purchases is an extremely profitable business.

In its early years, IBM Credit's operation was positively Dickensian. When an IBM field salesperson called in with a request for financing, he or she reached one of fourteen people sitting around a conference room table in Old Greenwich, Connecticut. The person taking the call logged the request for a deal on a piece of paper. That was step 1.

In step 2, someone carted that piece of paper upstairs to the credit department, where a specialist entered the information into a computer system and checked the potential borrower's creditworthiness. The specialist wrote the results of the credit check on the piece of paper and dispatched it to the next link in the chain, which was the business practices department.

The business practices department, step 3, was in charge of modifying the standard loan covenant in response to customer request. Business practices had its own computer system. When this task was completed, a person in that department would attach the special terms to the request form.

Next, the request went to a pricer, step 4, who keyed the data into a personal computer spreadsheet to determine the appropriate interest rate to charge the customer. The pricer wrote the rate on a piece of paper, which, with the other papers, was delivered to a clerical group, step 5.

There, an administrator turned all this information into a quote letter that could be delivered to the field sales representative by Federal Express.

The entire process consumed six days on average, although it sometimes took as long as two weeks. From the sales reps' point of view, this turnaround was too long, since it gave the customer six days to find another source of financing, to be seduced by another computer vendor, or simply to call the whole deal off. So the rep would call—and call and call—to ask, "Where is my deal, and when are you going to get it out?" Naturally, no one had a clue, since the request was lost somewhere in the chain.

In their efforts to improve this process, IBM Credit tried several fixes. They decided, for instance, to install a control desk so they could answer the rep's questions about the status of the deal. That is, instead of each department forwarding the credit request to the next step in the chain, it would return it to the control desk where the calls were originally taken. There, an administrator logged the completion of each step before sending the paper out again. This fix did indeed solve one problem: The control desk knew the location of each request in the labyrinth and could give the rep the information he or she wanted. Unfortunately, this information was purchased at the cost of adding more time to the turnaround.

Eventually, two senior managers at IBM Credit had a brainstorm. They took a financing request and walked it through all five steps, asking personnel in each office to put aside whatever they were doing and to process this request as they normally would, only without the delay of having it sit in a pile on someone's desk. They learned from their experiments that performing the actual work took in total only *ninety minutes*—one and a half hours. The remainder—now more than seven days on the average—was consumed by handing the form off from one department to the next. Management had begun to look at the heart of the issue, which was the overall credit issuance process. Indeed, if by the wave of some magic wand the company were able to double the personal productivity of each individual in the organization, total turnaround time would have been reduced by only forty-five minutes. The problem did not lie in the tasks and the people performing them, but in the structure of the process itself. In other words, it was the process that had to change, not the individual steps.

In the end, IBM Credit replaced its specialists—the credit checkers, pricers, and so on—with generalists. Now, instead of sending an application from office to office, one person called a deal structurer processes the entire application from beginning to end: No hand-offs.

How could one generalist replace four specialists? The old process design was, in fact, founded on a deeply held (but deeply hidden) assumption: that every bid request was unique and difficult to process, thereby requiring the intervention of four highly trained specialists. In fact, this assumption was false; most requests were simple and straightforward. The old process had been overdesigned to handle the most difficult applications that management could imagine. When IBM Credit's senior managers closely examined the work the specialists did, they found that most of it was little more than clerical: finding a credit rating in a database, plugging numbers into a standard model, pulling boilerplate clauses from a file. These tasks fall well within the capability of a single individual when he or she is supported by an easy-to-use computer system that provides access to all the data and tools the specialists would use.

IBM Credit also developed a new, sophisticated computer system to support the deal structurers. In most situations, the system provides the deal structurer with the guidance needed to proceed. In really tough situations, he or she can get help from a small pool of real specialists—experts in credit checking, pricing, and so forth.

Even here handoffs have disappeared because the deal structurer and the specialists he or she calls in work together as a team.

The performance improvement achieved by the redesign is extraordinary. IBM Credit slashed its seven-*day* turnaround to four *hours*. It did so without an increase in head count—in fact, it has achieved a small head-count reduction. At the same time, the number of deals that it handles has increased a hundredfold. Not 100 percent, but *100 times*.

What IBM Credit accomplished—a 90 percent reduction in cycle time and a hundredfold improvement in productivity—easily meets our definition of reengineering. The company achieved a *dramatic* performance breakthrough by making a *radical* change to the *process* as a whole. IBM Credit did not ask, "How do we improve the calculation of a financing quote? How do we enhance credit checking?" It asked instead, "How do we improve the credit issuance process?" Furthermore, in making its radical change, IBM Credit shattered the assumption that it needed specialists to perform specialized steps.

Ford Motor Company

Our second example of reengineering involves changes to a different category of process. We defined a process as a series of activities that delivers value to a customer and cited order fulfillment and credit issuance as examples. However, the customer of a process is not necessarily a customer of the company. The customer may be inside the company, as it is, for instance, for the materials acquisition or purchasing process, which supplies materials to a company's manufacturing operations. Reengineering can apply to these processes, too, as Ford Motor Company learned.

In the early 1980s, Ford, like many other American corporations, was searching for ways to cut overhead and administrative costs. One of the places Ford believed it could reduce costs was in its accounts payable department, the organization that paid the bills submitted by Ford's suppliers. At that time, Ford's North American accounts payable department employed more than 500 people. By using computers to automate some functions, Ford executives believed that they could attain a 20 percent head-count reduction in the department, bringing the number of clerks down to 400. By our definition, this incremental improvement, achieved by automating the existing manual process, would not qualify as business reengineering. Nonetheless, Ford managers thought 20 percent sounded pretty good—until they visited Mazda.

Ford had recently acquired a 25 percent equity interest in the Japanese company. The Ford executives noted that the admittedly smaller company took care of its accounts payable chores with only *five* people. The contrast—Ford's 500 people to Mazda's 5—was too great to attribute just to the smaller company's size, *esprit de corps*, company songs, or morning calisthenics. Automating to achieve a 20 percent personnel reduction clearly would not put Ford on a cost-par with Mazda, so the Ford executives were forced to rethink the entire process in which the accounts payable department took part.

This decision marked a critical shift in perspective for Ford, because companies can reengineer only business processes, not the administrative organizations that have evolved to accomplish them. "Accounts payable" cannot be reengineered, because it is not a process. It is a department, an organizational artifact of a particular process design. The accounts payable department consists of a group of clerks sitting in a room and passing paper amongst themselves. *They* cannot be reengineered, but what they *do* can be—and the way they are eventually reorganized to accomplish the new work process will follow from the requirements of the reengineered process itself.

We cannot emphasize this crucial distinction enough. Reengineering must focus on redesigning a fundamental business process, not on departments or other organizational units. Define a reengineering effort in terms of an organizational unit, and the effort is doomed. Once a real work process is reengineered, the shape of the organizational structure required to perform the work will become apparent. It probably will not look much like the old organization; some departments or other organizational units may even disappear, as they did at Ford.

The process that Ford eventually reengineered was not "accounts payable," but "procurement." That process took as input a purchase order from, say, a plant that needed parts and provided that plant (the process customer) with bought-and-paid-for goods. The procurement process included the accounts payable function, but it also encompassed purchasing and receiving.

Ford's old parts acquisition process was remarkably conventional. It began with the purchasing department sending a purchase order to a vendor, with a copy going to accounts payable. When the vendor shipped the goods and they arrived at Ford, a clerk at the receiving dock would complete a form describing the goods and send it to accounts payable. The vendor, meanwhile, sent accounts payable an invoice.

Accounts payable now had three documents relating to these goods—the purchase order, the receiving document, and the invoice. If all three matched, a clerk issued payment. Most of the time, that is what happened, but occasionally Vilfredo Pareto intervened.

Pareto, an early-twentieth-century Italian economist, formulated what most of us call the 80–20 rule, technically known as the law of maldistribution. This rule states that 80 percent of the effort expended in a process is caused by only 20 percent of the input. In the case of Ford's accounts payable department, clerks there spent the great majority of their time straightening out the infrequent situations in which the documents—purchase order, receiving document, and invoice—did not match. Sometimes, the resolution required weeks of time and enormous amounts of work in order to trace and clarify the discrepancies.

Ford's new accounts payable process looks radically different.

Accounts payable clerks no longer match purchase order with invoice with receiving document, primarily because the new process eliminates the invoice entirely. The results have proved dramatic. Instead of 500 people, Ford now has just 125 people involved in vendor payment.

The new process looks like this: When a buyer in the purchasing department issues a purchase order to a vendor, that buyer simultaneously enters the order into an on-line database. Vendors, as before, send goods to the receiving dock. When they arrive, someone in receiving checks a computer terminal to see whether the received shipment corresponds to an outstanding purchase order in the database. Only two possibilities exist: It does or it doesn't. If it does, the clerk at the dock accepts the goods and pushes a button on the terminal keyboard that tells the database that the goods have arrived. Receipt of the goods is now recorded in the database, and the computer will automatically issue and send a check to the vendor at the appropriate time. If, on the other hand, the goods do not correspond to an outstanding purchase order in the database, the clerk on the dock will refuse the shipment and send it back to the vendor.

The basic concept of the change at Ford is simple. Payment authorization, which used to be performed by accounts payable, is now accomplished at the receiving dock. The old process fostered Byzantine complexities: searches, suspense files, ticklers—enough to keep 500 clerks more or less busy. The new process does not. In fact, the new process comes close to eliminating the need for an accounts payable department altogether. In some parts of Ford, such as the Engine Division, the head count in accounts payable is now just 5 percent of its former size. Only a handful of people remains to handle exceptional situations.

The reengineered process at Ford breaks hard-and-fast rules that formerly applied there. Every business has these rules, deeply ingrained in the operation of the organization, whether they are explicitly spelled out or not.

For instance, rule 1 at Ford's accounts payable department was "We pay when we receive the invoice." While this rule was rarely articulated, it was the frame around which the old process was formed. When Ford's managers reinvented this process, they were effectively asking whether they still wanted to live by this rule. The answer was no. The way to break this rule was to eliminate invoices. Instead of "We pay when we receive the *invoice*," the new rule at Ford is, "We pay when we receive the *goods.*" Altering just that one word established the basis for a major business change. Other one-word changes in old rules at Ford are having similar effects today.

In one of its truck plants, for instance, instead of "We pay when we receive the goods," Ford has implemented an even newer rule: "We pay when we *use* the goods." The company has said in effect to one of its brake suppliers, "We like your brakes, and we will continue to install them on our trucks, but until we do, they are *your* brakes, not ours. The brakes only become ours when we use them, and that's when we'll pay for them. Every time a truck comes off the line with a set of your brakes on it, we'll mail you a check." This change has simplified even further Ford's purchasing and receiving procedures. (It also has paid off in other ways, from reducing inventory levels to improving cash flow.)

The new process for brake acquisition shatters another rule at Ford, the one that requires the company always to maintain multiple sources of supply. At least with regard to truck brakes, the new rule is, "We shall have a *single* source of supply and work *very* closely with that vendor."

One might wonder why the brake supplier agreed to this change, since it is now, for practical purposes, financing Ford's brake inventory. What benefit does the supplier derive from the new arrangement?

First, it now gets all of Ford's truck brake business instead of just some of it. Second, because the supplier is now privy to Ford's computerized manufacturing schedule, it does not have to depend on the unreliable forecasts of Ford's brake demands that it previously got from its own sales force. The brake supplier can better schedule its own production and reduce the size of its own inventory.

The reengineering of procurement at Ford illustrates another characteristic of a true reengineering effort: Ford's changes would have been impossible without modern information technology— which is likewise true for the reengineering effort at IBM Credit. The new processes at both companies are not just the old processes with new wrinkles. They are entirely new processes that could not exist without today's information technology.

In the reengineered procurement process, for example, Ford's receiving clerk could not authorize vendor payment when goods arrived without the on-line database of purchase orders. In fact, absent the database, the receiving clerk would be just as much in the dark as ever about what goods Ford had actually ordered. The clerk's only option when goods arrived would have been, as previously, to assume that they had been ordered, accept them, and leave it to accounts payable to reconcile the receiving document, the purchase order, and the invoice. In theory, purchasing could have sent a photocopy of every purchase order to every receiving dock in the company, and receiving clerks could have checked arriving goods against these, but for obvious reasons such a paper-based system would prove impractical. Technology has enabled Ford to create a radically new mode of operation. Similarly, at IBM Credit, technology permits generalists to have easy access to information previously available only to specialists.

We say that in reengineering, information technology acts as an *essential enabler.* Without information technology, the process could not be reengineered. We will return to this theme in Chapter 5.

Kodak

Another example of reengineering is the product development process that Kodak created in response to a competitive challenge. In 1987, Kodak's arch-rival, Fuji, announced a new 35mm, single-use camera, the sort that the customer buys loaded with film, uses once, and then returns to the manufacturer, who processes the film and breaks down the camera into parts for reuse. Kodak had no competitive offering, not even one in the works, and its traditional product design process would have taken seventy weeks to produce a rival to Fuji's camera. Such a time delay would have handed Fuji an enormous head start and advantage in a new market. To slash its time-to-market, Kodak reengineered its product development process.

Most product development processes are either sequential, which makes them slow, or parallel, which also makes them slow, but for a different reason. In a sequential development process, individuals or groups working on one part of a product wait until the previous step is completed before beginning their own. Camera body designers, for example, may do their work first, followed by shutter designers, then the film advance mechanism designers, and so on. It is no mystery why this process is slow.

In a parallel design process, all the parts are designed simultaneously and integrated at the end. But this method engenders its own problem: Usually, the subsystems will not fit together because, even though all the groups were working from the same basic camera design, changes—often improvements—occurred along the way but were not communicated to the other groups. Then, when the camera is supposed to be ready to go to production, it's back to square one in design.

Kodak's old product development process was partly sequential and partly parallel but entirely slow. Designing the camera was conducted in parallel, with that method's attendant problems, and the design of the manufacturing tooling was tacked on, sequentially, at the end. At Kodak, the manufacturing engineers did not even begin their work until twenty-eight weeks after the product designers had started.

Kodak reengineered its product development process through the innovative use of a technology called CAD/CAM—computer-aided design/computer-aided manufacturing. This technology allows engineers to design at computer workstations instead of at drafting tables. Just working at a screen instead of on paper would have made the designers individually more productive, but such use of the technology would have had only marginal effect on the process as a whole.

The technology that has enabled Kodak to reengineer its process is an integrated product design database. Each day this database collects each engineer's work and combines all the individual efforts into a coherent whole. Each morning, design groups and individuals inspect the database to see whether someone else's work yesterday has created a problem for them or for the overall design. If so, they resolve the problem *immediately*, instead of after weeks or months of wasted work. Moreover, this technology permits manufacturing engineers to begin their tooling design just ten weeks into the development process, as soon as the product designers have given the first prototype some shape.

Kodak's new process, called concurrent engineering, has been used widely in the aerospace and automotive industries and is now starting to attract adherents in consumer goods companies. Kodak exploited concurrent engineering to cut nearly in half—to thirty-eight weeks—the time required to move the 35mm, single-use camera from concept to production. Furthermore, because the reengineered process allows tooling designers to get involved before product design is finished, their expertise can be tapped to create a design that is more easily and inexpensively manufactured. Kodak has reduced its tooling and manufacturing costs for the single-use camera by 25 percent.

Recurrent Themes in Reengineering

In the three examples cited, we have seen illustrations of true business reengineering, even though some of them occurred before we had coined the term. These examples illustrate the four requisite characteristics of a reengineering effort and fulfill the definition that reengineering is the *fundamental* rethinking and *radical* redesign of business *processes* to achieve *dramatic* improvements in critical, contemporary measures of performance, such as cost, quality, service, and speed.

Several themes, listed below, emerge in these three cases, which we will explore at greater length later in this book.

- *Process orientation*. The improvements that IBM Credit, Ford, and Kodak effected did not come about by attending to narrowly defined tasks and working within predefined organizational boundaries. Each was achieved by looking at an entire process—credit issuance, procurement, and product development—that cut across organizational boundaries.

- *Ambition*. Minor improvements would not have been sufficient in any of these situations. All three companies aimed for breakthroughs. In reengineering its accounts payable process, Ford, for example, skipped the 20 percent fix and went for the 80 percent solution.

- *Rule-breaking*. Each of these companies broke with old traditions as they reengineered their processes. Assumptions of specialization, sequentiality, and timing were deliberately abandoned.

- *Creative use of information technology*. The agent that enabled these companies to break their old rules and create new process models was modern information technology. Information technology acts as an enabler that allows organizations to do work in radically different ways.

What Reengineering Isn't—And What It Is

People with hearsay knowledge of reengineering and those just being introduced to the concept often jump to the conclusion that it is much the same as other business improvement programs with which they are already familiar. "Oh, I get it. Reengineering," they may say, "is another name for downsizing." Or they equate it with restructuring or some other business fix of the month. Not at all. Reengineering has little or nothing in common with any of these other programs and differs in significant ways even from those with which it does share some common premises.

First, despite the prominent role played by information technology in business reengineering, it should by now be clear that reengineering is not the same as automation. Automating existing processes with information technology is analogous to paving cow paths. Automation simply provides more efficient ways of doing the wrong kinds of things.

Nor should people confuse business reengineering with so-called software reengineering, which means rebuilding obsolete information systems with more modern technology. Software reengineering often produces nothing more than sophisticated computerized systems that automate obsolete processes.

Reengineering is not restructuring or downsizing. These are just fancy terms for reducing capacity to meet current, lower demand. When the market wants fewer GM cars, GM reduces its size to better match demand. But downsizing and restructuring only mean doing less with less. Reengineering, by contrast, means doing *more* with less.

Reengineering also is not the same as reorganizing, delayering, or flattening an organization, although reengineering may, in fact, produce a flatter organization. As we have argued above, the problems facing companies do not result from their *organizational* structures but their *process* structures. Overlaying a new organization on top of an old process is pouring soured wine into new bottles.

Companies that earnestly set out to "bust" bureaucracies are holding the wrong end of the stick. Bureaucracy is not the problem. On the contrary, bureaucracy has been the solution for the last 200 years. If you dislike bureaucracy in your company, try getting by without it. Chaos will result. Bureaucracy is the glue that holds traditional corporations together. The underlying problem, to which bureaucracy has been and remains a solution, is that of fragmented processes. The way to eliminate bureaucracy and flatten the organization is by reengineering the processes so that they are no longer fragmented. Then the company can manage nicely without its bureaucracy.

Nor is reengineering the same as quality improvement, total quality management (TQM), or any other manifestation of the contemporary quality movement. To be sure, quality programs and reengineering share a number of common themes. They both recognize the importance of processes, and they both start with the needs of the process customer and work backward from there. However, the two programs also differ fundamentally. Quality programs work within the framework of a company's existing processes and seek to enhance them by means of what the Japanese call *kaizen,* or continuous incremental improvement. The aim is to do what we already do, only to do it better. Quality improvement seeks steady incremental improvement to process performance. Reengineering, as we have seen, seeks breakthroughs, not by enhancing existing processes, but by discarding them and replacing them with entirely new ones. Reengineering involves, as well, a different approach to change management from that needed by quality programs.

Finally, we can do no better than to return to our original two-word definition for reengineering: starting over. Reengineering is about beginning again with a clean sheet of paper. It is about rejecting the conventional wisdom and received assumptions of the past. Reengineering is about inventing new approaches to process structure that bear little or no resemblance to those of previous eras.

Fundamentally, reengineering is about reversing the industrial revolution. Reengineering rejects the assumptions inherent in Adam Smith's industrial paradigm—the division of labor, economies of scale, hierarchical control, and all the other appurtenances of an early-stage developing economy. Reengineering is the search for new models of organizing work. Tradition counts for nothing. Reengineering is a new beginning.

CHAPTER 3

RETHINKING BUSINESS PROCESSES

It should be clear by now that a reengineered business process looks vastly different from a traditional process. But what, exactly, does a reengineered process look like?

We can't give a single answer to this question, because reengineered processes take many different forms. Nonetheless, we can say a great deal about the characteristics that typify reengineered processes.

As we've observed and participated in reengineering projects at dozens of corporations, we've noticed striking similarities among their various reengineered processes, similarities that transcend industry type and even the identity of the particular process. Much of what holds true for an auto company that has reengineered its processes is also true for an insurance company or a retailer.

That recurring themes appear in companies that have undergone reengineering should not come as a surprise, since the shape of a company that has reengineered, like the shape of the traditional industrial organization, flows from a small set of fundamental premises. The industrial model rests on the basic premise that workers have few skills and little time or capacity for training. This premise inevitably requires that the jobs and tasks assigned to these workers be very simple. Moreover, Adam Smith argued that people work most efficiently when they have only one easily understood task to perform. Simple tasks, though, demand complex processes to knit them all together, and for 200 years companies have accepted the inconvenience, inefficiencies, and costs associated with complex processes in order to reap the benefits of simple tasks.

In reengineering, we stand the industrial model on its head. We say that in order to meet the contemporary demands of quality, service, flexibility, and low cost, processes must be kept simple. This need for simplicity has enormous consequences for how processes are designed and organizations are shaped.

Here, then, are some commonalities, some recurring themes or characteristics, that we frequently encounter in reengineered business processes.

• Several jobs are combined into one

The most basic and common feature of reengineered processes is the absence of an assembly line; that is, many formerly distinct jobs or tasks are integrated and compressed into one. We observed this characteristic at IBM Credit, where several specialist jobs, such as credit checker or pricer, were combined into a single position, "deal structurer." We encountered a similar transformation at an electronics company that had reengineered its order fulfillment process. Previously, specialists located in separate organizations performed each of the five steps between selling and installing the company's equipment. Because this process involved so many handoffs, errors and misunderstandings were inevitable—all the more so because no one individual or group had responsibility for, or knowledge of, the entire process. When customers telephoned with problems, no one could help them.

In reengineering this process, the company compressed responsibility for the various steps and assigned it to one person, the "customer service representative." That person now performs the whole process and also serves as the single point of contact for the customer. Our term for such an individual responsible for an end-to-end process is *case worker*.

It is not always possible to compress all the steps in a lengthy process into one integrated job performed by a single person. In some situations (product delivery, for example), the various steps must be performed in different locations. In those instances, a company needs several people, each managing parts of the process. In other cases, it may not prove practical to teach one person all the skills he or she would need to perform the entire process.

Bell Atlantic, for example, found that it was too much to ask one person to handle all the tasks involved in establishing high-speed digital circuits for business customers. But the company also wanted to do away with the problems that inevitably occurred when the order was passed between people across departmental lines. To eliminate the handoffs, Bell Atlantic organized what we call a *case team*, a group of people who have among them all the skills that are needed to handle an installation order.

Case team members—who previously were located in different departments at several geographic locations—were brought together into a single unit and given total responsibility for installing the equipment. While handoffs between team members may still create some delays and errors, they are insignificant compared to the problems that the cross-organizational handoffs caused. Perhaps most important, everyone now knows who has responsibility for getting an order processed quickly and accurately.

The payoffs of integrated processes, case workers, and case teams can be enormous. Eliminating handoffs means doing away with the errors, delays, and rework that they engender. Typically, a case worker–based process operates *ten times* faster than the assembly line version that it replaces. Bell Atlantic, forerunner of Verizon, for example, reduced the time it takes to install a high-speed digital service link from thirty days to three; in some instances, it now takes only several hours. Moreover, because the new process generates fewer errors and misunderstandings, the company doesn't need additional people to find and fix them.

Integrated processes have also reduced process administration overheads. Because employees involved in the process assume responsibility for making sure that customers' requirements are met on time and with no defects, they need less supervision. Instead, the company encourages these empowered employees to find innovative and creative ways to reduce cycle time and cost continually while producing a defect-free product or service. Improved control is another benefit of integrated processes; because they involve fewer people, assigning responsibility for them and monitoring performance is easier.

• Workers make decisions

Companies that undertake reengineering not only compress processes horizontally, by having case workers or case teams perform multiple, sequential tasks, but vertically as well. Vertical compression means that at the points in a process where workers used to have to go up the managerial hierarchy for an answer, they now make their own decisions. Instead of being separated from real work, decision making becomes *part* of the work. Workers themselves now do that portion of a job that was formerly performed by managers.

Under the mass-production paradigm, the tacit assumption is that the people actually performing work have neither the time nor the inclination to monitor and control it and that they lack the depth and breadth of knowledge required to make decisions about it. The industrial practice of building hierarchical management structures follows from this assumption. Accountants, auditors, and supervisors check, record, and monitor work. Managers supervise the worker bees and handle the exceptions. This assumption, and its consequences, need to be discarded.

The benefits of compressing work vertically as well as horizontally include fewer delays, lower overhead costs, better customer response, and greater empowerment for workers.

• The steps in the process are performed in a natural order
Reengineering processes are freed from the tyranny of straight-line sequence; natural precedence in the work, rather than the artificial one introduced by linearity, can be exploited. Typically, in a conventional process, person 1 must complete task 1 before passing the results to person 2 to do task 2. But what if task 2 could be performed simultaneously with task 1? Linear sequencing of tasks imposes an artificial precedence that slows work down.

In reengineered processes, work is sequenced in terms of what needs to follow what. In one manufacturing company, for example, it took five steps to go from the receipt of a customer order to the installation of the equipment. The first step was to determine the customer's requirements; the second, to translate them into internal product codes; the third, to convey the coded information to various plants and warehouses; the fourth, to receive and assemble the components; and the fifth, to deliver and install the equipment. A different organization performed each step.

Traditionally, group 1 completed step 1 before group 2 began step 2, but this was not actually necessary. The employee responsible for step 1 spent most of her time gathering information that would not be required until step 5. Because of the arbitrary linear sequencing imposed on the process, however, no one could begin working on step 2 until step 1 was completed. In the reengineered version of this process, step 2 begins as soon as step 1 has collected enough information to get it started. Then while steps 2, 3, and 4 operate, step 1 continues to collect the information needed for step 5. As a result, the company reduced the time it takes to fill a customer order by more than 60 percent.

We have already encountered another example of a process freed from strict linearity with Kodak's new product development process. There, design of the manufacturing tooling does not have to wait until product design is finished. As soon as the basic product design is in place, tooling engineers can not only begin their work, they can influence the rest of the product design process.

"Delinearizing" processes speeds them up in two ways. First, many jobs get done simultaneously. Second, reducing the amount of time that elapses between the early and late steps of a process narrows the window for major change that might make the earlier work obsolete or the later work inconsistent with the earlier. Organizations thereby encounter less rework, which is another major source of delay.

• Processes have multiple versions

We might term the fourth common characteristic of reengineered processes the end of standardization. Traditional processes were intended to provide mass production for a mass market. All inputs were handled identically, so companies could produce uniform and consistent outputs. In a world of diverse and changing markets that logic is obsolete. To meet the demands of today's environment, we need multiple versions of the same process, each one tuned to the requirements of different markets, situations, or inputs. What's more, these new processes must have the same economies of scale that result from mass production.

Processes with multiple versions or paths usually begin with a "triage" step to determine which version works best in a given situation. Triage is at work at IBM Credit, which has put in place three versions of the credit issuance process: one for straightforward cases (which are performed entirely by computer), one for medium hard cases (performed by the deal structurer), and one for difficult cases (performed by the deal structurer with help from specialist advisers).

We know a man who, in order to make some minor improvement to his house, had to wait six months for a public hearing before a city board that, when it finally considered his application, took only twenty seconds to approve it. His application, illustrated by a hand-drawn sketch, had to travel through the same process as those of multimillion-dollar office tower developers with volumes of blueprints, plans, and materials specification sheets. If the city had reengineered its building permit system, it might have replaced the single process with two or maybe three processes: one for small projects, one for big projects, and one for those in the middle. Simple triage, based on some preestablished thresholds, would have sent our friend's application quickly and efficiently through the right one.

Traditional one-size-fits-all processes are usually very complex, since they must incorporate special procedures and exceptions to handle a wide range of situations. A multiversion process, by contrast, is clean and simple, because each version needs to handle only the cases for which it is appropriate. There are no special cases and exceptions.

• Work is performed where it makes the most sense
A fifth recurring theme in reengineered processes is the shifting of work across organizational boundaries. In traditional organizations, work is organized around specialists—and not just on the factory floor. Accountants know how to count and purchasing clerks know how to order things, so when the accounting department needs new pencils, the purchasing department buys them. Purchasing finds vendors, negotiates price, places the order, inspects the goods, and pays the invoice—and eventually the accountants get their pencils, unless the approved supplier is short on pencils and purchasing decides to substitute pens.

This kind of process is expensive, since it involves a variety of departments plus the overhead that's associated with tracking all the paper and fitting all the pieces of the process together. One company we know ran a controlled experiment and learned that it expended $100 in internal costs to buy $3 worth of batteries. It also discovered that 35 percent of its purchase orders were for amounts less than $500.

The notion of spending $100 internally to expend $500 or less did not sit well, so the company decided to off-load the responsibility for purchasing goods onto the process customers; in other words, the accountants—as well as everyone else—now buy their own pencils. They know from whom to buy and what to pay, because purchasing has negotiated these prices and given the accountants a list of approved vendors. Each operating unit has a credit card with a $500 credit limit. At the end of the month, the bank that issued the credit card sends the manufacturer a tape of all the card transactions, which the company then runs against its internal general ledger system so that the accountants' budget gets charged for their pencils.

As a result, the requesters receive their products more quickly and with less hassle and the company spends far less than $100 on the processing costs. This example illustrates what we mean when we say that the customer of a process can perform some or all of the process in order to eliminate handoffs and overhead and cut costs.

In an analogous way, an electronics equipment manufacturer reengineered its field service process by shifting some of the repair work to its customers, who now make simple fixes themselves without having to wait for a technician to arrive with, maybe, the right spare parts. Some spare parts are now stored at each customer's site and managed through a computerized parts management system. When a problem crops up, the customer calls the manufacturer's field service hot line and describes the symptoms to a diagnostician, who can ask a computer for help. If the problem is something the customer can fix, the diagnostician tells the customer what part to replace and how to install it. Later, the manufacturer picks up the old part and leaves a new part in its place. Service technicians make site calls only when the problem is too complex for the customer.

Sometimes, though, it's more effective when the supplier to a customer process performs some or all of the process on behalf of the customer. Navistar International, for example, has shifted some of its work back to its suppliers. Instead of managing its own warehouse inventory of tires to be installed on the trucks it manufactures, Navistar has turned warehouse management over to Goodyear, which has more expertise than Navistar at managing tire warehouses. Goodyear sees that Navistar gets the Goodyear, Bridgestone, and Michelin tires it needs as it needs them.

For Navistar, this shift is the ultimate in process simplification: The manufacturer no longer has to manage its tire inventory at all. Since Goodyear, the supplier, is much better than Navistar, the customer, at warehouse management, the amount of inventory in the warehouse has dropped from twenty-two days' supply to five.

In other words, in the aftermath of reengineering, the correspondence between processes and organizations may look very different from how it looked beforehand. Work is shifted across organizational boundaries to improve overall process performance. Much of the work done in organizations consists of integrating related pieces of work that independent organizational units perform. Relocating work across organizational boundaries, as exemplified in the cases above, eliminates the need for this integration.

• Checks and controls are reduced

Another kind of nonvalue-adding work that gets minimized in reengineered processes is checking and control; or, to put it more precisely, reengineered processes use controls only to the extent that they make economic sense.

Conventional processes are replete with checking and control steps, which add no value but are included to ensure that people aren't abusing the process. In a typical purchasing process, for example, the purchasing department checks the signature of the person requesting an item to make sure that person is authorized to acquire the requisitioned goods in the dollar amount specified and verify that the department's budget is good for the bill. All this checking is to make sure that people in the organization are not buying items that they should not.

While that objective may be laudable, many organizations fail to recognize the costs associated with strict control. It takes time and labor to do all this checking; in fact, it may take more time and effort to do the checking than to do the actual purchasing. Worse, the cost of the checking may even exceed the cost of the goods being purchased.

Reengineered processes exhibit a more balanced approach. Instead of tightly checking work as it is performed, reengineered processes often have aggregate or deferred controls. These control systems will, by design, tolerate modest and limited abuse, by delaying the point at which abuse is detected or by examining aggregate patterns rather than individual instances. The reengineered control systems, however, more than compensate for any possible increase in abuse by dramatically lowering the costs and other encumbrances associated with the control itself.

Consider the credit card–based purchasing process we just described. Compared to more traditional processes, this one seems almost devoid of controls. Departments might use their credit cards to go on wild spending sprees. People could run away to Brazil with the spoils of their raids on office supply vendors. Or so the company's internal auditors feared. But they were wrong because the reengineered purchasing process does have a point of control; unauthorized purchases will be detected when the credit card tape is run against the department's budget and when the departmental manager reviews the expenditures. Given the credit limit on the cards, the process designers felt it was better to swallow the limited exposure to abuse that the new process embodies in order to eliminate the overhead cost associated with the traditional controls. (We should keep in mind, as well, that the old process was far from immune to abuse.)

Some automobile insurance companies are taking similar approaches in their claims processing activities. Traditionally, insurers dispatch claims adjusters and appraisers to assess the extent of auto damage and determine how much the insurer is willing to pay for repair. This control step is designed to make sure that the body shop performing the repair doesn't inflate the bill or do unnecessary work. But adjusters aren't inexpensive, and they slow the process down, thereby antagonizing claimants—and angry claimants often sue.

Consequently, some insurers take adjusters out of the process for small accidents. They send the claimant to an approved body shop and say they will pay for whatever needs to be done. How do they avoid overbilling? By periodically reviewing the body shop's charges, the insurer can get a sense of the pattern of its repairs and compare them against normative standards and patterns of other body shops. A shop that is doing too many front-end alignments, say, will get a warning: If you continue this abuse, you'll get dropped from the approved list and get no more referrals from us. The insurance companies are happy to accept the potential of some short-term abuse, because the cost will be more than offset by the benefits of a streamlined claims process that is less expensive to operate and leaves claimants happy.

• Reconciliation is minimized

Yet another form of nonvalue-adding work that reengineered processes minimize is reconciliation. They do it by cutting back the number of external contact points that a process has, thereby reducing the chances that inconsistent data requiring reconciliation will be received. The accounts payable process at Ford, described in Chapter 2, illustrates this principle.

Ford's old accounts payable process contained three points of contact with vendors: at the purchasing department through the purchase order, at the receiving dock through the receiving paperwork, and at accounts payable through the invoice. Three points of contact meant enormous opportunities for inconsistency; the purchase order could disagree with either the receiving document or the invoice, and either of them could disagree with the other. By eliminating the invoice, Ford reduced the points of external contact from three to two and the opportunity for inconsistency by two-thirds. As a result, the checking and reconciliation work that accounts payable had heretofore performed became unnecessary, which meant that the accounts payable organization could shrink dramatically.

This theme and several others are illustrated in the way Wal-Mart, working with Procter & Gamble, reengineered the management of its Pampers inventory. Pampers, a disposable diaper, is a bulky item that requires a lot of storage space relative to its dollar value. Wal-Mart maintained Pampers inventory at its distribution centers, from which it filled orders coming from the stores. When the distribution center inventory began to run low, Wal-Mart would reorder more diapers from P&G.

Managing inventory is a delicate balancing act. Too little inventory makes for unhappy customers and lost sales. Too much incurs high financing and storage costs. Not only that, inventory management is itself a costly activity. With the idea of improving this aspect of its business, Wal-Mart approached P&G with the observation that P&G probably knew more about diaper movement through warehouses than Wal-Mart, as it had information about usage patterns and reorders from retailers all over the country. Wal-Mart suggested, therefore, that P&G should assume the responsibility of telling Wal-Mart when to reorder Pampers for its distribution center and in what quantity. Every day, Wal-Mart would tell P&G how much stock it was moving out of the distribution center to the stores. When P&G felt it was appropriate, it would tell Wal-Mart that it was time to reorder and how much. If the recommendation seemed to make sense, Wal-Mart would approve it, and P&G would ship the goods.

The new arrangement worked so well that over time Wal-Mart suggested that P&G henceforth skip the purchase recommendations and just ship the diapers it thought Wal-Mart would need. In other words, Wal-Mart off-loaded its inventory replenishment function onto its supplier, illustrating the principle of relocating work across organizational boundaries that we discussed earlier. In this case, though, the boundaries were *inter*company, not *intra*company. Both companies reap advantages.

Wal-Mart has eliminated the costs associated with maintaining its Pampers inventory. The stock is managed more effectively, since P&G indeed can do a better job than Wal-Mart. Therefore, the retailer has less inventory on hand and suffers fewer out-of-stock situations. Lower inventory levels free up space in Wal-Mart's distribution center and reduce the retailer's need for working capital to finance that inventory. In fact, inventory management is now so streamlined that goods move through Wal-Mart's distribution center and stores and into the hands of the consumer even before Wal-Mart has to pay P&G for the goods. When it does pay, Wal-Mart is using cash it has already received from consumers. Whether we call this arrangement negative inventory carrying costs or an infinite return on capital, it is a wonderful state of affairs for Wal-Mart.

Anyone could provide diapers to Wal-Mart, but P&G adds value to the diapers it supplies by performing the inventory management process. It thereby endears itself as a preferred supplier to the large retail chain. As a preferred supplier, P&G gets additional shelf space in Wal-Mart stores and the much sought after end-aisle displays. The reengineered process also has major internal performance benefits for P&G. First, the company can run its manufacturing and logistics operations more efficiently now that it has the information it needs to better project product demand. Inventory no longer moves to Wal-Mart irregularly in large lots, but continually in small ones. Other manufacturer-retailer combinations, such as Levi Strauss and many of its customers, also use this approach, known as "continuous replenishment."

The second benefit P&G reaps from its new arrangement with Wal-Mart relates back to the notion of minimizing the number of external contact points—in this case, in P&G's accounts receivable process. Conventionally, accounts receivable's job is to reconcile payments from customers with customer orders and with the vendor's own invoices. In principle they should match, but reality does not always follow principle. When they do not—as, for example, when prices have recently changed—these conflicts vanish into the black hole of reconciliation, where they consume enormous energy and damage the vendor-customer relationship. P&G, however, now has only two accounts receivable contacts with Wal-Mart: the invoice and the payment. Wal-Mart no longer generates the original order; P&G does. In this way, errors and the need for reconciliation are enormously reduced.

• A case manager provides a single point of contact

The use of someone we might call a "case manager" is another recurring characteristic we find in reengineered processes. This mechanism proves useful when the steps of a process either are so complex or are dispersed in such a way that integrating them for a single person or even a small team is impossible. Acting as a buffer between the still complex process and the customer, the case manager behaves with the customer as if he or she were responsible for performing the entire process, even though that is really not the case.

To perform this role—that is, to be able to answer the customer's questions and solve customer problems—the case manager needs access to all the information systems that the people actually performing the process use and the ability to contact those people with questions and requests for further assistance when necessary.

We sometimes call the case managers "empowered" customer service representatives to distinguish them from traditional CSRs, who are often people with skimpy information and less clout. Empowered CSRs can actually get things done. At Duke Power Company, a large public utility based in Charlotte, North Carolina, case managers present customers with the useful fiction of an integrated customer service process by handling all their problems while shielding them from the real complexities of the actual process.

• Hybrid centralized-decentralized operations are prevalent

Companies that have reengineered their processes have the ability to combine the advantages of centralization and decentralization in the same process. We will encounter this theme at Hewlett-Packard in Chapter 5, where a standard purchasing system and a shared database allow the company to combine the best of both worlds.

Information technology increasingly enables companies to operate as though their individual units were fully autonomous, while the organization still enjoys the economies of scale that centralization creates. Equipping field sales representatives with notebook computers connected by wireless modems to the central office or to corporate headquarters, for instance, gives salespeople instant access to information that is maintained there. At the same time, controls incorporated into the software they use to write up sales contracts prevent the salespeople from quoting unreasonable prices or specifying delivery or other conditions that the organization cannot meet. With this technology, companies can reengineer the sales process so as to eliminate the bureaucratic machinery of regional field offices, enhance the sales representatives' autonomy and empowerment, and, simultaneously, improve the control the company has over selling prices and conditions.

Many banks have established separate divisions to sell different products to the same clients—large corporations, for instance. One division sells traditional lines of credit; another, asset-based finance; a third, letters of credit; and a fourth, pension fund management services. The decentralized structure ensures that each division focuses on the products and services with which it has the most expertise and simultaneously promotes real entrepreneurial autonomy. It also guarantees chaos.

In this fractionalized structure, everyone is looking at narrow slices of the market, but no one is looking at the customer as a whole, so important aggregate issues may fall between the cracks. One bank, for example, established a $20 million credit limit for a certain customer and instructed each autonomous unit to enforce it. Each one did—by extending the client the full $20 million credit. The bankwide exposure to the client was therefore many times that figure. Management only understood its true exposure after the client went bankrupt. To avoid these kinds of problems, several banks have implemented bankwide customer databases that all operating units share. Every unit puts what they know about the customer and their relationship with that customer into the database, and every unit uses the database as a source of customer information. In this way, units with freedom to act independently can coordinate their activities without the bureaucratic interference of a central control point.

The objective of presenting the above examples and of pointing out the characteristics that we see recurring in reengineered business processes is not to suggest that all reengineered processes look the same or that process redesign is a straightforward matter. Nothing could be further from the truth. Not every reengineered business process will display all of the characteristics we have cited. Indeed, they could not, because some are conflicting. Actually creating a new design requires insight, creativity, and judgment. These ingredients are also needed for designing the jobs and organizations that support reengineered processes. This is the topic we next turn our attention to.

CHAPTER 4

THE NEW WORLD OF WORK

We have repeatedly made the point that reengineering entails the radical redesign of a company's business processes. But while reengineering does start with process redesign, it doesn't end there. Fundamental changes in business processes have implications for many other parts and aspects of an organization—every part of it, in fact.

When a process is reengineered, jobs evolve from narrow and task-oriented to multidimensional. People who once did as they were instructed now make choices and decisions on their own instead. Assembly-line work disappears. Functional departments lose their reasons for being. Managers stop acting like supervisors and behave more like coaches. Workers focus more on the customers' needs and less on their bosses'. Attitudes and values change in response to new incentives. Practically every aspect of the organization is transformed, often beyond recognition.

Let's look closer at the kinds of changes that occur when a company reengineers its business processes.

• Work units change—from functional departments to process teams

Companies that reengineer are, in effect, putting back together again the work that Adam Smith and Henry Ford broke into tiny pieces so many years ago. Once it is restructured, process teams—groups of people working together to perform an entire process—turn out to be the logical way to organize the people who perform the work. Process teams don't contain representatives from all the functional departments involved. Rather, process teams *replace* the old departmental structure. While there are several different kinds of process teams, we mean something very particular when we use the word "team."

Think of the progress of an order (or a new product idea or an insurance claim) through an organization. Each of these items gets handled by many different people, but those people are not organizationally integrated. They are scattered all over the company in functional silos—different departments, groups, divisions, and so on. This fractionation creates numerous problems, but in particular it promotes incongruent goals among the different people involved. One person might care about inventory turns, while another is focused on delivery time.

An alternative approach is to look at the same collection of people who are now handling the order or new product or claim, but instead of separating them into departments, put them together in a team. We aren't necessarily changing what they do, but we're arranging for them to do it together instead of separately, scattered all over the organization. In some sense we're only putting back together a group of workers who have been artificially separated by organization. When they're rejoined, we call them a process team. A process team, in other words, is a unit that naturally falls together to complete a whole piece of work—a process.

Process teams are of many sorts, the right one depending on the nature of the work being done. One we call a *case team*. Here, as we saw with Bell Atlantic in the last chapter, a number of people with different skills work together to complete routine, recurring work—such as processing an insurance claim or connecting a telephone customer to its long-distance carrier. In the past, when a Bell Atlantic business customer requested a connection between its telephone system and a long-distance carrier for data services, for instance, the request traveled from department to department at Bell Atlantic, taking from two weeks to one month to complete its journey. In reengineering that process, Bell Atlantic took people from many functional departments and put them together in case teams, which now handle most customer requests in a matter of days or even hours instead of weeks. Because case teams perform recurring work—that is, they process similar customer requests day after day—the people on the team are usually permanently grouped together. (We will look more closely at the Bell Atlantic example in Chapter 13.)

Another kind of a process team has a shorter life span, because it stays together only for as long as it takes to complete a particular episodic task. We call these *virtual teams*. Kodak's new product design process, for instance, requires many people with diverse talents—shutter designers, lens specialists, manufacturing experts, and others—to work jointly on a new camera design project. When the camera is designed and goes into production, however, the project is finished and the virtual team dissolves, its members moving on to other projects and other teams. People may simultaneously be members of more than one virtual team, splitting their time among different projects.

IBM Credit (which we first looked at in Chapter 2) uses a third kind of process team. It's like a case team, but it consists of only one person. Prior to reengineering, when IBM Credit put together a financing package for a prospective customer, credit checking was done in the credit department, pricing was done in the pricing department, other terms and conditions were set in the business practices department, and the final offer got pulled together by someone in the bid preparation department. People in these departments passed the work back and forth among themselves, with all the usual errors and delays. But when the company reengineered its deal-structuring process, it integrated those four separate functions, replacing four departments with one. Many of the people—called deal structurers—who staff this new department are the same people who used to be specialists.

IBM Credit went further than simply grouping four specialists into a process team. Now, each individual can shepherd an entire deal through the process from beginning to end. IBM Credit realized that one trained person with access to on-line data could handle 90 percent or more of the work that used to get handed off among specialists. A few specialist advisers assigned to assist deal structurers could help them handle the rest. At IBM Credit, the process team is a team of one—what we have called a *case worker*.

• Jobs change—from simple tasks to multidimensional work
People working on process teams will find their work far different from the jobs to which they've been accustomed. Assembly-line work, whether it's of the white- or blue-collar variety, is highly specialized—the repetitious performance of one task. The job may require some training—how to insert a particular component into a particular printed circuit board, for instance. It may even require extensive education—a college degree in mechanical engineering in order to design camera shutters. But when they're doing task work, neither the assembly-line worker nor the mechanical engineer needs to know—or even cares much about—the whole process of, say, building a computer or developing a camera design.

Process team workers, who are collectively responsible for process results rather than individually responsible for tasks, have a different kind of job. They share joint responsibility with their team members for performing the whole process, not just a small piece of it. They not only use a broader range of skills from day to day, they have to be thinking of a far bigger picture. While not every member of the team will be doing exactly the same work—after all, they have different skills and abilities—the lines between them blur. Each team member will have at least a basic familiarity with all the steps in the process and is likely to perform several of them. Moreover, everything an individual does is imbued with an appreciation for the process as a whole.

A clear example of how jobs change after reengineering is provided by IBM Credit. The old jobs consisted of specialists who did one task. The new deal structurers perform a variety of tasks. They are generalists. Their work is multidimensional.

What happened at Kodak when the company reengineered its product design process? A lens designer who used to concentrate strictly and narrowly on lens design now designs lenses in the context of the camera as a whole, which means that he or she inevitably contributes to other aspects of the design and that his or her own design will be influenced by what others have to say. The lens no longer operates strictly within the limits of one designer. The job has become multidimensional.

Sometimes process reengineering shifts the boundaries between different kinds of work. At one company, for instance, engineers who previously had prepared data for other people to use in producing marketing brochures now produce the marketing brochures themselves; they know more about the product than the marketing people, and they are able to use the desktop publishing tools themselves. The marketing people now act as advisers to the engineers. Work for both groups—the engineers and the marketing people—has broadened.

As work becomes more multidimensional, it also becomes more substantive. Reengineering eliminates not just waste but non-value-adding work as well. Most of the checking, reconciling, waiting, monitoring, tracking—the unproductive work that exists because of boundaries within an organization and to compensate for process fragmentation—is eliminated by reengineering, which means that people will spend more time doing *real* work.

After reengineering, work becomes more satisfying, since workers achieve a greater sense of completion, closure, and accomplishment from their jobs. They actually perform a whole job—a process

or a subprocess—that by definition produces a result that somebody cares about. Process performers share many of the challenges
and rewards of entrepreneurs. They are focused on customers
whose satisfaction is their aim. They're not just trying to keep the
boss happy or to work through the bureaucracy.

Moreover, work becomes more rewarding since people's jobs
have a greater component of growth and learning. In a process team
environment, personal development does not mean climbing up
through the hierarchy but expanding one's breadth—learning more
so one can encompass a larger part of the process. After reengineering there is no such thing as "mastering" a job; as a worker's expertise and experience grow, his or her job grows with it.

Moreover, since workers in reengineered processes spend more
time on value-adding work and less time on work that adds no
value, their contributions to the company increase, and, consequently, jobs in a reengineered environment will on the whole be
more highly compensated.

There is, however, a challenging side to all this good news about
work in a reengineered environment. If jobs are more satisfying,
they are also more challenging and difficult. Much of the old, routine work is eliminated or automated. If the old model was simple
tasks for simple people, the new one is complex jobs for smart people, which raises the bar for entry into the workforce. Few simple,
routine, unskilled jobs are to be found in a reengineered environment.

• People's roles change—from controlled to empowered
A task-oriented, traditional company hires people and expects them
to follow the rules. Companies that have reengineered don't want
employees who can follow rules; they want people who will make
their own rules. As management invests teams with the responsibility of completing an entire process, it must also give them the
authority to make the decisions needed to get it done.

The following example illustrates the nature and payoff of

empowerment. A guest approached the doorman at a major hotel and complained that his radar detector had been stolen from his car in the hotel's garage. The doorman, empowered to perform customer service, asked how much it cost, took the guest to the front desk, and said to the clerk, "Give this man $150." Everybody gulped, but the customer was satisfied. Two weeks later, the general manager received a letter from this customer that stated he had found his radar detector in his trunk. In the envelope was also a check for $150. The postscript to the letter added: "By the way, I will never stay at any other hotel chain for the rest of my life."

People working in a reengineered process are, of necessity, empowered. As process team workers they are both permitted and required to think, interact, use judgment, and make decisions. At IBM Credit and Kodak, intrusive supervisors and managers have no place in the reengineered work processes. Imagine an IBM Credit deal structurer who is trying to handle several cases in different stages of completion and to get as many of them done as quickly as possible. Suddenly, a supervisor appears to check on his or her progress. Real work screeches to a halt while the deal structurer shifts to satisfying the supervisor instead of the customer. At Kodak, when could the head of the lens department "approve" the lens design? The lens design isn't final until the camera design is done. Supervisory approval would only slow the process.

Teams, of one person or several, performing process-oriented work are inevitably self-directing. Within the boundaries of their obligations to the organization—agreed-upon deadlines, productivity goals, quality standards, etc.—they decide how and when work is going to be done. If they have to wait for supervisory direction of their tasks, they aren't process teams.

Empowerment is an unavoidable consequence of reengineered processes; processes can't be reengineered without empowering process workers. Consequently, companies that reengineer must consider additional criteria in their hiring. It is no longer enough merely to look at prospective employees' education, training, and skills; their *character* becomes an issue as well. Are they self-start-ing? Do they have self-discipline? Are they motivated to do what it takes to please a customer?

Reengineering and its consequent empowerment have powerful implications for the kinds of people companies will hire.

• Job preparation changes—from training to education
If jobs in reengineered processes require that people not follow rules but rather exercise judgment in order to do the right thing, then employees need sufficient education to discern for themselves what that right thing is. Traditional companies typically stress employee *training*—teaching workers how to perform a particular job or how to handle one specific situation or another. In companies that have reengineered, the emphasis shifts from training to *educa-tion*—or to hiring the educated. Training increases skills and compe-tence and teaches employees the "how" of a job. Education increases their insight and understanding and teaches the "why."

Hill's Pet Products, a subsidiary of Colgate-Palmolive, recently built a new plant in Richmond, Indiana, at which the company has implemented many of the principles of reengineered processes. The company's management knew the kind of people they needed to work on the plant floor and set out to hire 150 of them. The com-pany received thousands of applications and the personnel depart-ment looked closely at 3,000. When the finalists were selected, practically all of them shared one characteristic: They lacked factory work experience. The applicants who the company wanted mostly turned out to be former schoolteachers, police officers, and others who had the right character and the right education. Their lack of factory skills, an ostensible deficit, wasn't a major problem. The company was able to train the new hires because these were people who already knew how to learn.

For multidimensional and changing jobs, companies don't need people to fill a slot, because the slot will be only roughly defined. Companies need people who can figure out what the job takes and do it, people who can create the slot that fits them. Moreover, the slot will keep changing. In an environment of flexibility and change, it is clearly impossible to hire people who already know everything they're ever going to need to know, so continuing education over the lifetime of a job becomes the norm in a reengineered company.

• Focus of performance measures and compensation shifts—from activity to results

Worker compensation in traditional companies is relatively straightforward: People are paid for their time. In a traditional operation—whether it's on an assembly line manufacturing machines or in a clerical office processing paperwork—an individual employee's work has no quantifiable value. What, for instance, is the dollar value of a soldered joint? Or of verified employment data on an insurance application form? Neither is worth anything by itself. Only the finished car or the newly issued insurance policy has value to the company. When work is fragmented into simple tasks, companies have no choice but to measure workers on the efficiency with which they perform narrowly defined work. The trouble is that increased efficiency of narrowly defined tasks does not necessarily translate into improved process performance.

In contrast, the IBM Credit deal structurer is not measured by how many pieces of paper he or she handles but by the number and profitability of finalized deals and by their quality, as reflected in customer satisfaction surveys. When employees are performing process work, companies can measure their performance and pay them on the basis of the value they create. That value is measurable because in reengineered business processes, teams create products or services that have intrinsic value. A new camera, for instance, has value; a shutter mechanism does not.

Reengineering also forces companies to reconsider some basic assumptions about compensation. For instance, an employee's performance in a reengineered job this year does not guarantee anything about his or her performance in the years to come. For that reason, base salaries in companies with reengineered processes tend to remain relatively flat after adjustments for inflation. Substantial rewards for outstanding performance take the form of bonuses, not pay raises.

Other compensation assumptions also fall away after reengineering: paying people based on job rank or seniority; paying people just for showing up; and giving people a raise just because another year has passed.

Paying people based on their position in the organization—the higher up they are, the more money they make—is inconsistent with the principles of reengineering. Traditional point schemes, in which the size of a person's salary is a function of the number of subordinates that person has working for him or her and the size of his or her budget, also don't fit in a process-oriented environment. Finely graded hierarchies with a lot of positions—analyst 1, analyst 2, senior analyst, etc.—each with a narrow compensation band, must be discarded.

In companies that have reengineered, contribution and performance are the primary bases for compensation. Precedents for this approach exist: Even in traditional companies, the vice president of sales is rarely the most highly paid person in the sales organization—that honor usually belongs to the most productive sales rep. On Wall Street, the chairman of an investment bank is typically not the most highly paid individual; rather, it is usually the star bond dealer or currency trader.

In companies that have reengineered, performance is measured by value created, and compensation should be set accordingly.

• Advancement criteria change—from performance to ability
A bonus is the appropriate reward for a job well done. Advancement to a new job is not. In the aftermath of reengineering, the distinction between advancement and performance is firmly drawn. Advancement to another job within the organization is a function of ability, not performance. It is a change, not a reward.

Progressive Insurance considers this distinction important

enough to note in the company's annual report. "One of our core principles," the document says, "is that we pay for performance and promote for ability." Once considered, the principle seems obvious. But it is rarely followed. If Elizabeth is a good chemist, conventional thinking goes, she will be a good manager of chemists. Often that isn't true, and Elizabeth's "promotion" could get the company a bad manager at the cost of a good chemist.

Capital Holding's Direct Response Group, an insurer, makes the distinction between performance and advancement quite clear to its employees. "We've separated the results review, at which we reward people with compensation, from the development review," says DRG senior vice president Pamela Godwin. "This way, we can even get people who may have delivered outstanding results to acknowledge their need for additional growth and development. By separating the two evaluations we help keep the differences clear in employees' minds."

• Values change—from protective to productive
Reengineering entails as great a shift in the culture of an organization as in its structural configuration. Reengineering demands that employees deeply believe that they work for their customers, not for their bosses. They will believe this only to the extent that the company's practices of reward reinforce it. For instance, Xerox Corporation doesn't just tell its people that customers pay their salaries, it makes the connection explicit. The company now bases a major portion of every manager's bonus on a measure of customer satisfaction. When their bonuses depended solely on how well their individual departments performed, managers continually warred with one another over fault, jurisdiction, and resources. Now, the internal arguments have all but disappeared as managers have shifted their focus to maximizing customer satisfaction.

An organization's management systems—the ways in which people are paid, the measures by which their performance is evaluated, and so forth—are the primary shapers of employees' values and beliefs.

Unfortunately, too many managers still believe that all they have to do to shape their employees' belief systems is to articulate some high-sounding values and then make speeches about them. Creating a corporate value statement alone is useless and just another faddish exercise. Without supporting management systems, most corporate value statements are collections of empty platitudes that only increase organizational cynicism. To be worth the paper it's printed on, a value statement must be reinforced by the company's management systems. The statement articulates values; the management systems give those values life and reality within the company.

And, of course, senior management must live these values themselves. If an executive says it's important to care about customers and then spends an hour a week on the phone with customers, the value of that time to customers may be minor, but its value to the organization is immeasurable. The hour is a symbol and a demonstration of management's personal commitment to the values by which they expect everyone to live.

The cultural values found in some traditional companies are the by-products of fragmented management systems, which focus on past performance, emphasize control, and enshrine the hierarchy. Whatever such a company's value statement might *say*, its management systems may in fact promote values something like this:

• My boss pays my salary. For all the talk about serving customers, the real objective is to keep the boss happy.

• I'm just a cog in the wheel. My best strategy is to keep my head down and not make waves.

• The more direct reports I have, the more important I am. The one with the biggest empire wins.

• Tomorrow will be just like today. It always has been.

The trouble is that these values and beliefs do not promote the performance that customer-oriented organizations require. They are inconsistent with the new processes created in a reengineered environment, and unless the values change, new processes, no matter how well designed, will never work. Changing values is as important a part of reengineering as changing processes.

In a company that has reengineered, employees must hold beliefs such as the following:

- Customers pay all our salaries. I must do what it takes to please them.
- Every job in this company is essential and important. I do make a difference.
- Showing up is no accomplishment. I get paid for the value I create.
- The buck stops here. I must accept ownership of problems and get them solved.
- I belong to a team. We fail or we succeed together.
- Nobody knows what tomorrow holds. Constant learning is part of my job.

- Managers change from supervisors to coaches

When a company reengineers, once complex processes become simpler while once simple jobs grow complex. For instance, the process of getting a deal put together at IBM Credit has gone from one that entails four or five different people to one that involves just a single person: A deal structurer does the whole thing. Consequently, the company's managers now have to spend less time keeping the pieces of paper moving through departments but more time helping employees do richer and more demanding work.

Process teams, consisting of one person or many, don't need bosses; they need *coaches*. Teams ask coaches for advice. Coaches help teams solve problems. Coaches are not *in* the action, but they are close enough to it to assist the team in its work.

Traditional bosses design and allocate work. Teams do that for themselves. Traditional bosses supervise, monitor, control, and check work as it moves from one task performer to the next. Teams do that themselves. Traditional bosses have little to do in a reengineered environment. Managers have to switch from supervisory roles to acting as facilitators, as enablers, and as people whose jobs are the development of people and their skills so that those people will be able to perform value-adding processes themselves.

This kind of managing is a real profession. Traditional practice undervalues both work and management. It undervalues work by stating that the only way a worker can get ahead is by becoming a manager. Managing, this implies, is more important than working. But the traditional practice also says that anybody who does well as a worker can manage.

In fact, managing is a particular skill, just like engineering or sales, and there is little correlation between excelling in a work skill and being a good manager. Casey Stengel was an adequate baseball player; he was a great manager. Most great players have made lousy managers.

Managers in a reengineered company need strong interpersonal skills and have to take pride in the accomplishment of others. Such a manager is a mentor, who is there to provide resources, to answer questions, and to look out for the long-term career development of the individual. This is a different role from the one most managers have traditionally played.

• Organizational structures change—from hierarchical to flat
When a whole process becomes the work of a team, process management becomes part of the team's job. Decisions and interdepartmental issues that used to require meetings of managers and managers' managers now get made and resolved by teams during the course of their normal work. Pushing decisions about work down to the people doing it means that managers' traditional roles are diminished. Companies no longer require as much managerial "glue" as they used to in order to hold work together. After reengineering it no longer takes all the king's horses and all the king's men

to put fragmented processes back together again. With fewer managers there are fewer management layers.

In the traditional company, organizational structure is an important issue on which enormous amounts of energy are expended. Why? Because organizational structure is the mechanism through which a great many issues get resolved and questions get answered.

Remember that the basic unit of the traditional organization is the functional department, a collection of people performing similar tasks. The organization as a whole consists of these functional departments arranged in various ways. The arrangements vary widely among companies. In the so-called functional company, all related functional departments are aggregated into a single functional division: All sales departments come together in a sales division. In a structure based on strategic business units, functional departments are grouped together by markets, so a company might have an institutional division or a West Coast division, for instance.

A lot of energy goes into designing these organizations because the shape of the organization determines much about it, from how the company's work is organized to the mechanisms for the exercise of control and performance monitoring. The organizational structure establishes the lines of communication within the organization and determines the decision-making hierarchy.

In companies that have reengineered, however, organizational structure isn't such a weighty issue. Work is organized around processes and the teams that perform them. Lines of communication? People communicate with whomever they need. Control is vested in the people performing the process.

Consequently, whatever organizational structure remains after reengineering tends to be flat, as work is performed by teams of essentially coequal people operating with great autonomy and supported by a few managers—few, because while a manager can typically supervise only about seven people, he or she can coach close to thirty. At a manager-worker ratio of 1 to 7, an organization is of necessity hierarchical. At a ratio of 1 to 30, it is much less so.

When asked about his postreengineering organizational chart, Stephen Israel, a senior vice president at IBM Credit, replied, "We have one, but we never look at it." The structure of his organization has become, in a phrase, "A bunch of people doing work." Such a company does not rely on its structure per se to answer many questions. After reengineering the issue of structure is considerably diminished in importance.

• Executives change—from scorekeepers to leaders
Not the least of the changes set off by reengineering is the opportunity and necessity for a shift in the role of a company's senior executives. Flatter organizations move senior executives closer to customers and to the people performing the company's value-adding work. In a reengineered environment, the successful accomplishment of work depends far more on the attitudes and efforts of empowered workers than on the actions of the task-oriented functional managers. Therefore, executives must be leaders who can influence and reinforce employees' values and beliefs by their words and their deeds.

Executives have overall responsibility for reengineered process performance without having direct control over the people performing them. These people are working more or less autonomously with the guidance of their coaches. Executives fulfill their responsibilities by ensuring that processes are designed in such a way that workers can do the job required and are motivated by the company's management systems—the performance measurement and compensation systems—to do it.

In traditional companies executives are divorced from operations. Their perspective on the companies they run is primarily a financial one: Did the company make its numbers this quarter? As leaders in a company that has reengineered, they move closer to the real work. In shaping processes and providing workers with motivation, they're intimately concerned with how the work gets done. No football coach tells the team, "I want you to win by fifteen points.

Get in there and play, and at the end of the game, report to me how it comes out." Although coaches don't play, they're closely involved in creating the game plan and in the players' performance. So is the executive in a reengineered company. They are far more than just scorekeepers.

Let us summarize the changes that occur when a company reengineers its business processes: Jobs certainly change, as do the people needed to fill them, the relationships those people have with their managers, their career paths, the ways people are measured and compensated, the roles of managers and executives, and even what goes on in workers' heads. In short, reengineering a company's business processes ultimately changes practically everything about the company, because all these aspects—people, jobs, managers, and values—are linked together. We call them the four points of the business system diamond. The top point on the diamond is the way the work gets done—the company's business processes; the second is its jobs and structures; the third, its management and measurement systems; and the fourth, its culture—what its employees value and believe.

The Business System Diamond

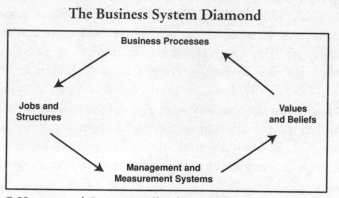

The linkages are key. The top point of the business system diamond, processes, determines the second point, jobs and structures.

The ways in which work is performed determine the nature of people's jobs and how the people who perform these jobs are grouped and organized. The fragmented processes found in traditional companies lead to narrowly specialized jobs and organizations based on functional departments. Integrated processes give rise to multidimensional jobs that are best organized into process teams.

Likewise, people who perform multidimensional jobs and who are organized into teams must be recruited, evaluated, and paid by means of appropriate management systems. In other words, jobs and structures, themselves determined by the process designs, in turn lead to the third point on the diamond, the kind of management systems a company must have.

The management systems—how people are paid, the measures by which their performance is evaluated, and so forth—are the primary shapers of employees' values and beliefs, the fourth point on the diamond. By values and beliefs, we mean the issues and concerns that people in the organization think are important and to which they pay significant attention.

Finally, the reigning values and beliefs in an organization must support the performance of its process designs. For example, an order fulfillment process that is designed to operate quickly and accurately will not do so unless the people performing it believe speed and accuracy are important. This brings us back to the top of the diamond. Once again we say that in reengineering it is not sufficient to redesign processes alone. All four points on the business system diamond have to fit together or the company will be flawed and misshapen.

The fact is that every company, even those with traditional organizations, has a business diamond. Reengineering can be thought of as replacing a diamond that has lost its luster and brilliance with a new one.

There is one part of reengineering that we have touched on but not yet discussed. That is the role that information technology plays. It is integral, and the next chapter explains why.

CHAPTER 5

THE ENABLING ROLE OF INFORMATION TECHNOLOGY

A company that cannot change the way it thinks about information technology cannot reengineer. A company that equates technology with automation cannot reengineer. A company that looks for problems first and then seeks technology solutions for them cannot reengineer.

Information technology plays a crucial role in business reengineering, but one that is easily miscast. State-of-the-art information technology is part of any reengineering effort, an *essential enabler* as we termed it in Chapter 2, since it permits companies to reengineer business processes. But, to paraphrase what is often said about money and government, merely throwing computers at an existing business problem does not cause it to be reengineered. In fact, the misuse of technology can block reengineering altogether by reinforcing old ways of thinking and old behavior patterns. Consider what throwing computers at the problem might have accomplished at the three companies, IBM Credit, Ford, and Kodak, whose reengineering efforts we examined in Chapter 2.

IBM Credit might have tried to accelerate its tortuously slow turnaround of credit applications by computer-linking the five different species of specialists who processed each one of them. Such a system would have accelerated the old process by eliminating the time required to move pieces of paper from one specialist's office to another. It would have done nothing, however, to eradicate the far greater queue time that awaited the forms when they arrived at each office. By computerizing the process, the company might have achieved a 10 percent performance improvement instead of the more than 90 percent improvement it attained through reengineering.

Ford, too, might have simply computerized its vendor payment process. By doing so, company executives estimated they would have been able to do away with 20 percent of the 500 jobs in the accounts payable unit. Instead, by reengineering the process, they eliminated 80 percent of those jobs.

Kodak could have shaved a few days from product and tooling design by giving its product and tooling designers state-of-the-art CAD workstations, but it would never have obtained the almost 50 percent reduction in overall product development time that it achieved by reengineering the process.

Learning to Think Inductively

To recognize the power inherent in modern information technology and to visualize its application requires that companies use a form of thinking that businesspeople usually don't learn and with which they may feel uncomfortable. Most executives and managers know how to think *deductively*. That is, they are good at defining a problem or problems, then seeking and evaluating different solutions to it. But applying information technology to business reengineering demands *inductive* thinking—the ability to first recognize a powerful solution and then seek the problems it might solve, problems the company probably doesn't even know that it has.

Ford managers originally thought their problem was to find a method for processing vendor invoices quicker and with fewer people. What they found instead was a solution that let them do away with invoices entirely. IBM Credit's executives thought their problem was how to speed the movement of information among various groups of specialists. Information technology allowed the company to eliminate the specialists so that it did not need to move the information around at all. Kodak thought its problem was pushing designers to work faster so that succeeding design steps could start sooner. Its technology solution virtually eliminated the need for sequential design.

The fundamental error that most companies commit when they look at technology is to view it through the lens of their existing processes. They ask, "How can we use these new technological capabilities to enhance or streamline or improve what we are already doing?" Instead, they should be asking, "How can we use technology to allow us to do things that we are *not* already doing?" Reengineering, unlike automation, is about innovation. It is about exploiting the latest capabilities of technology to achieve entirely new goals. One of the hardest parts of reengineering lies in recognizing the new, unfamiliar capabilities of technology instead of its familiar ones.

Even Thomas J. Watson, Sr., the founder of IBM, fell victim to this common shortsightedness when he proclaimed that the world-wide demand for data-processing computers would come to fewer than fifty machines. Twenty years later, mainframe computer makers and corporate computer managers both dismissed the minicomputer as a toy. Ten years after that, the personal computer received the same reception: "We're already meeting our needs with large machines," the conventional thinking went, "so why would we need small ones?" The answer, as we can see now, was that the great power of minicomputers, and then of PCs, did not lie in doing what larger machines already did but in giving birth to entirely new classes of applications.

Thinking deductively about technology not only causes people to ignore what is really important about it, it also gets them excited about technologies and applications that are, in fact, trivial and unimportant. Not long ago, for instance, someone thought it would be a terrific idea to integrate the personal computer and the telephone. The integrated unit would save space on desktops and be less expensive than buying separate units. That may be true, but combining the two machines into one doesn't offer any breakthroughs in capability. It doesn't let people do important things that they couldn't do before. It was at best a marginal improvement.

A lack of inductive thinking about technology is not a new problem, nor one confined to laypeople. Early on, many people thought that the greatest potential for the telephone lay in reducing the loneliness of the farmer's wife. Thomas Edison once said he thought the value of the phonograph, which he invented, was its ability to allow "dying gentlemen" to record their last wishes. Marconi, the developer of the radio, viewed it as a wireless telegraph that would operate point-to-point; he didn't recognize its potential as a broadcast medium. The real power of xerography was completely missed by no less a company than IBM.

In the late 1950s, when Xerox was performing the basic research on the 914, its first commercial copying machine, the company was hard-pressed for money and wanted to cash out of the project. It offered its patents to IBM, which hired Arthur D. Little (ADL), the Cambridge, Massachusetts–based consulting firm, to do a market research study. ADL concluded that even if the revolutionary machine captured 100 percent of the market for carbon paper, dittograph, and hectograph—the techniques used for copying documents at the time—it still would not repay the investment required to get into the copier business. IBM, on the best evidence available, decided to turn down the Xerox patents and stay out of copiers. Despite the downbeat forecast, Xerox decided to persevere, on the assumption that *someone* would find a use for the machines.

We know now—indeed, it seems obvious—that the power of the

Xerox copier did not lie in its ability to replace carbon paper and other existing copying technologies, but in its ability to perform services beyond the reach of these technologies. The 914 created a market for convenience copies that had previously not existed. Thirty copies of an existing document to share with a group of coworkers was not a need people knew they had before the invention of xerography. Since people couldn't make thirty easily and inexpensively, no one articulated doing so as a "need."

What we see operating in these cases of technology creating its own previously undreamed of uses is a variant of Say's law. Jean Baptiste Say, an early-nineteenth-century French economist, observed that in many situations, supply creates its own demand. People do not know they want something until they see that they can have it; then they feel they can't live without it. Alan Kay, often referred to as the father of the personal computer and now Apple Fellow at Apple Computer, puts it this way: "An important technology first creates a problem, and then solves it." No one "needed" the 914 copier—no one knew that they had a problem it solved—until the 914 appeared. Then the latent, unarticulated need suddenly became tangible and overwhelming.

It is, therefore, no use simply asking people how they would use a technology in their business. They will inevitably reply in terms of how that technology might improve a task they do already. One can usefully inquire of people whether they prefer their milk in glass bottles or cardboard cartons. Consumers are familiar with milk and with the two types of containers, and they can provide good information about their preferences and the reasons for them. If, though, a market researcher were to ask people in the prexerography days about copy machines, as they did, the respondents would say that it was hardly worth the price just to replace carbon paper.

Similarly, if a market research firm asks a person who travels frequently on business what would make his life easier, he might reply that he would like a faster way to reach the airport, or might express a yearning for a private plane. What he will *not* say he needs is a Star

Trek–style teleportation device. He won't, because such a device is outside his frame of reference. When the market researcher mentions business travel to him, the business traveler's mind thinks of the familiar process: Get stuck in traffic on the way to the airport, stand in line, scrunch into seat, eat terrible food. Those are the problems of which he is aware and the ones to which he will seek solutions. The true power of technology is to offer answers to problems he does not know he has—how to eliminate air travel completely, for example.

Sony Corporation has achieved a good measure of its success by paying attention to this fundamental precept—that market research done for a product that does not yet exist is useless. When Sony developers first envisioned the Walkman, management did not order up a market research survey to see if the product would be embraced by consumers. Realizing that people are unable to conceptualize what they do not know, Sony gave the Walkman the green light based on developers' insights into people's needs and the capabilities of the technology. The Walkman transformed, rather than responded to, people's ideas about where and how they could listen to music.

The larger point we want to make is that needs, as well as aspirations, are shaped by people's understanding of what is possible. Breakthrough technology makes feasible activities and actions people have not yet dreamed of. The challenge that most corporations fail to meet is recognizing the business possibilities that lie latent in technology. This shortcoming is understandable if not excusable.

Take, for instance, teleconferencing. This technology allows people located in specially equipped rooms in remote locations to hear and see each other and to work together almost as though they were in the same room. Initially, most organizations saw the value of teleconferencing as a means of reducing travel costs; people would be able to meet without having to fly. In this respect, teleconferencing has, by and large, proved a monumental failure. People travel to be with other people for many reasons. A trip, whether it's across town or across the country, in its very undertaking says something about the importance attached to the message ultimately delivered, of the subject eventually discussed. The nonverbal communication that takes place in a face-to-face meeting is probably more important than most of the words actually spoken. No surprise, then, that teleconferencing has had little effect on corporate travel costs.

That doesn't mean, however, that teleconferencing is without value. It means that its worth lies in transforming how work is done, not in lowering its costs. For instance, one company we know has used teleconferencing to cut its product development cycle by six months. How?

This company's engineering and marketing staffs are based in two different states, so once a month one group would fly to the other's location and they would iron out their problems face-to-face. Now the company has installed teleconferencing facilities, but the engineers and marketers still fly to see one another once a month, because they have found it difficult to resolve all their differences over television. The medium is too cool, and teleconferencing is no substitute for hand-to-hand combat. However, the engineers and marketers do use teleconferencing for weekly discussion sessions, which, previously, they could not hold because of the inconvenience, lost time, and costs associated with travel.

During their weekly teleconferences, the two groups can follow up on the points they discussed at the last face-to-face meeting. Moreover, they can include more people in their discussions. Before teleconferencing, the senior managers were too busy to devote three days—one day to get there, one day to meet, and one day to get home—to a monthly meeting, and it proved too expensive to buy airline tickets for the junior staff involved in the projects. That meant that only the midlevel people met face-to-face. With teleconferencing, everyone can "meet" once a week, stay informed, and have his or her routine questions answered. As a result, product developers and marketers keep in better touch, problems get resolved earlier and faster, fewer trips get taken down blind alleys, projects are completed faster, and the products they produce are better suited to their markets.

In short, the value of teleconferencing to this company lay in allowing it to do something it had *not* done before: keep marketers and designers in weekly contact. This use had not occurred to the people promoting teleconferencing, because they had not broken out of their old, deductive thinking mode.

To reiterate, the real power of technology is not that it can make the old processes work better, but that it enables organizations to break old rules and create new ways of working—that is, to reengineer.

In building a brand-new facility in which to manufacture its Saturn cars, General Motors enjoyed the opportunity to reengineer old work processes without the constraints imposed on it by existing plants. Consequently, GM, which had great ambitions for the Saturn facility, could break rules in a wholesale fashion by capitalizing on the enabling capabilities of information technology.

GM designed the Saturn plant, located in Spring Hill, Tennessee, to include an on-line manufacturing database that can be accessed by the company's component suppliers. The suppliers do not wait for GM to send them a purchase order; they simply consult the car maker's production schedule, which is included in the database. Then they take it upon themselves to deliver the appropriate parts to the assembly plant as needed. By knowing how many cars GM plans to make in the following month, for instance, the company supplying Saturn's brakes knows how to configure its own production and shipping schedule. It is the brake manufacturer's responsibility to show up at 8:30 in the morning at the right door at the right plant with the right brakes for the right cars, palletized in line-sequence order. Nobody at Saturn has to instruct the vendor explicitly to do so.

In this process, there is no paper—no purchase order and no invoice. After the parts are shipped, the vendor sends an electronic message to Saturn saying, in effect, "These are the parts we have sent to you." When the box of goods arrive, the receiving clerk scans the bar code printed on it with an electronic wand. The computer can then tell the receiving clerk what part of the plant the goods should go to. The scanning also initiates payment to the vendor.

In essence, information technology—in this case, the production schedule database and electronic data interchange (EDI)—has enabled Saturn and its supplier to operate as one company, to eliminate overhead in both organizations, and to break one of the oldest rules in any corporation's unwritten rule book: Treat vendors as adversaries.

In fact, breaking rules is how we recommend that people learn to think inductively about technology during the reengineering process: Find the long-standing rule or rules that technology allows the company to break, then see what business opportunities are created by breaking those rules. Teleconferencing, for example, breaks the rule that remotely located people can meet only infrequently and at great cost. Now it's possible for those people to meet often and inexpensively in an environment where limitations of geographical separation no longer count.

That insight gives a company a powerful tool for transforming its operations. It is one that can be applied in many areas and to many processes, not just to product development. Several mass merchandisers, such as Wal-Mart and Kmart, are using teleconferencing to allow headquarters-based merchandisers to provide store managers in the field with guidance and advice. Teleconferencing enables them to combine local initiative with centralized expertise.

IBM Credit, Ford, and Kodak used technology to break rules as well. The rules, explicit or not, were neither frivolous nor absurd when they were first articulated. They were expressions of the wisdom people had derived from experience. A smart plant manager runs short of parts only a few times because of unexpected demand before he learns to order a little extra. In the absence of forecasting technology, this practice makes perfect sense. But the advent of that technology breaks the reigning rule about the need for safety stocks to buffer demand.

It is this *disruptive* power of technology, its ability to break the rules that limit how we conduct our work, that makes it critical to companies looking for competitive advantage.

Following are some illustrations of additional rules about the organization of work that can be broken by various information technologies, some of them familiar and some state of the art.

Old rule: Information can appear in only one place at one time
Disruptive technology: Shared databases
New rule: Information can appear simultaneously in as many
    places as it is needed

It is sobering to reflect on the extent to which the structure of our business processes has been dictated by the limitations of the file folder. When information is captured on paper and stored in a folder, only one person can use it at a time. Making copies and distributing them is not always feasible and, in any event, leads to the creation of multiple and eventually inconsistent versions of the file. Consequently, work involving this information tends to be structured sequentially, with one individual completing his or her tasks, then passing the folder to the next in line.

Database technology changes this rule. It allows many people to use the information simultaneously.

In an insurance business, for instance, clerk A can be calculating an applicant's premium rate while clerk B checks his or her credit—both of them using the same application form—since neither job depends upon the other. By allowing one document to exist in several places at once, database technology can free a process from the artificial limitations of sequencing.

Old rule: Only experts can perform complex work
Disruptive technology: Expert systems
New rule: A generalist can do the work of an expert

When expert systems technology appeared on companies' radar screens in the early 1980s, most envisioned its utility in straightforward and simplistic terms. They would exploit it to automate the work of highly sophisticated experts by capturing their expertise in computer software. This was an extraordinarily foolish idea for several reasons: The technology is not really up to it; we need to retain the experts anyway, so they can continue to learn and advance in their field; and it is not clear why such clever people would participate in sharing all their knowledge with a computer designed to replace them.

In time, though, more sophisticated organizations have learned that there is more money in not being dumb than in being smart. That is, the real value of expert systems technology lies in its allowing relatively unskilled people to operate nearly at the level of highly trained experts.

A major chemical company, for example, has given each of its customer service representatives an expert system that advises them on product features and relationships. This system has allowed each of them to treat every customer inquiry as a cross-selling opportunity, something that previously only the very best had done.

Generalists supported by integrated systems can do the work of many specialists, and this fact has profound implications for the ways in which we can structure work. As illustrated by the changes at IBM Credit, systems technology allows the introduction of a case worker, who can handle all steps in a process from beginning to end. By eliminating the handoffs, delays, and errors inherent in a traditional sequential process, a case worker–based process can achieve order-of-magnitude improvements in cycle time, accuracy, and cost.

Old rule: Businesses must choose between centralization and
    decentralization
Disruptive technology: Telecommunications networks
New rule: Businesses can simultaneously reap the benefits of
    centralization and decentralization

Businesspeople "know" that manufacturing plants, service facilities, and sales offices located far from headquarters must be treated as separate, decentralized, autonomous organizations if they are to function effectively and efficiently. Why? Because if every question that cropped up in the field had to be referred back to headquarters for an answer, little would get accomplished—and even that little would be late. Experience teaches that people in the field generally work best if they can make their own decisions.

If companies are relying on old technologies—the U.S. mail, the telephone, or even overnight express—to move their information back and forth, they must sacrifice central management control in order to achieve flexible and responsive field operations.

New technologies, however, free companies from this trade-off. High-bandwidth communications networks allow headquarters to have the same information that field offices have and to see the data that field offices see—and vice versa—in real time. With this shared capability, every field office can effectively be part of headquarters, and headquarters can be part of every field office. That means companies can utilize whatever arrangement—centralization, decentralization, or some combination—best serves their markets.

Information technology enabled Hewlett-Packard, the Palo Alto, California–based designer and manufacturer of instruments and computer systems, to break the time-honored rule that centralization and decentralization are mutually exclusive.

In materials procurement, as in most of its activities, Hewlett-Packard was highly decentralized. It granted its operating divisions virtually complete autonomy in purchasing, because they knew their own needs best. But the virtues of decentralization (flexibility, customization, responsiveness) are purchased at a cost (lack of economies of scale and reduced control). At Hewlett-Packard, decentralized purchasing meant that the company could not take advantage of high-volume discounts available from its vendors. For that reason, Hewlett-Packard estimated that it was spending $50 to $100 million more each year than necessary on raw materials. Centralizing purchasing would not have "solved" the problem of high cost; it would merely have exchanged it for the twin problems of unresponsiveness and bureaucracy. Instead, Hewlett-Packard found a third way, through the use of a common purchasing software system.

Under Hewlett-Packard's new approach, each manufacturing division continues to order parts for its division. Now, however, each purchasing unit uses a standard purchasing system. These systems all provide data to a new database, which a corporate procurement unit oversees. Corporate procurement negotiates block contracts and volume discounts with suppliers of selected products on behalf of Hewlett-Packard as a whole. Corporate procurement can do so, because the database gives the unit complete information about the divisions' planned and actual purchases. Once contracts are established, purchasing agents check the database to locate approved suppliers and place orders.

The new process gives Hewlett-Packard the best of centralization—volume discounts—and the best of decentralized buying—meeting local needs locally.

Information technology, used imaginatively, has eliminated the need for separate, fully formed field units with their own overheads, and the banking industry, for one, has already begun to recognize this reality. For years, banks treated branches as P & L (Profit & Loss) centers, but now many banks see a branch only as a point of sale and not as a self-contained organization. The availability of automated teller machines and other high-capacity, real-time data network devices means that branch transactions show up in the central bank's books immediately. Since a branch now becomes just a point of sale, banks can keep people close to the customer without having to relinquish central control of operations.

Old rule: Managers make all decisions

Disruptive technology: Decision support tools (database access, modeling software)

New rule: Decision making is part of everyone's job

Part of the industrial revolution model is the notion of hierarchical decision making. The worker performing a task is expected only to do the job, not to think or make decisions about it. These prerogatives are reserved for management. These rules were not simply manifestations of industrial feudalism. Managers did in fact have broader perspectives, based on more information, than did lower-level workers. This better information presumably allowed them to make superior decisions.

The costs of hierarchical decision making, however, are now too high to bear. Referring everything up the ladder means decisions get made too slowly for a fast-paced market. Today, companies say they realize that frontline workers must be empowered to make their own decisions, but empowerment cannot be achieved simply by giving people the authority to make decisions. They need the tools as well.

Modern database technology allows information previously available only to management to be made widely accessible. When accessible data is combined with easy-to-use analysis and modeling tools, frontline workers—when properly trained—suddenly have sophisticated decision-making capabilities. Decisions can be made more quickly and problems resolved as soon as they crop up.

Old rule: Field personnel need offices where they can receive, store, retrieve, and transmit information

Disruptive technology: Wireless data communication and portable computers

New rule: Field personnel can send and receive information wherever they are

---

With wideband, wireless data communications and portable computers, field people of whatever occupation can request, view, manipulate, use, and transmit data almost anywhere without ever having to run back to the office.

Wireless data communication relies on technology similar to that used in cellular telephones, with the important difference that it allows users to send data instead of, or in addition to, voice. With increasingly miniaturized terminals and computers, people can connect to information sources wherever they are. Otis Elevator's service people, for instance, carry with them small portable terminals. After they repair an elevator, they update the customer's service record on the spot, then send the information via modem to headquarters in Connecticut. Avis has applied the same principle to its rental operations. When a customer returns a car to an Avis lot, an attendant, equipped with a tiny computer, meets the car, pulls up the record of the rental transaction, and enters the charge. The customer never has to visit the office.

Earlier, we noted that high-bandwidth communication lets companies break the old rule that says field offices must be autonomous organizations. Wireless data communication goes further and begins to eliminate the need for field offices entirely. Processes such as job progress reporting, insurance claims adjusting, and on-site equipment repair consultation will not depend upon a field-worker's having to find a phone or a computer terminal. Headquarters can know what the people on-site know when they know it—and vice versa.

Old rule: The best contact with a potential buyer is personal
 contact
Disruptive technology: Interactive videodisk
New rule: The best contact with a potential buyer is effective
 contact

Some companies have started using interactive videodisks, which allow viewers to watch a video segment on a computer screen and then ask questions or answer them on screen. The initial application of this technology was in training, but the potential power of interactive video far transcends this domain.

Several retailers, for example, are experimenting with interactive video to augment their retail sales force. Customers at these stores can select a product from a menu, watch a video presentation about it, ask questions, then order it with a credit card—all without human intervention. The process may seem cold and impersonal, but customers find it preferable to the usual retail experience: waiting forever for a salesperson only to discover that he or she is uninformed.

Banks have begun using interactive video to explain their increasingly complex services to customers, who can ask the machine to clarify points that they don't understand. Some information is *best* communicated visually—real estate, for instance. Interactive video gives prospective buyers a tour of entire houses—and lets them return to see the master bedroom again if they ask—without their having to leave the broker's office.

Old rule: You have to find out where things are
Disruptive technology: Automatic identification and tracking
 technology
New rule: Things tell you where they are

Combined with wireless data communication, automatic identification technology lets things—trucks, for instance—tell you constantly where they are. You do not have to look for them, and when you want them to go someplace else, they get the word instantaneously. No more waiting for drivers to hit the next truck stop so they can telephone the dispatcher.

A company that knows in real time where its trucks are, or railcars or service technicians for that matter, does not need as many of them. It does not require as much redundancy in personnel, equipment, and materials to cover the delays inherent in locating and rerouting things and people in transit.

Some railroads, for instance, are implementing satellite systems to tell them where a given train is at any given moment. The old method of tracking trains involved painting bar code–like symbols on the sides of the railcar. As the train pulled through the station, a machine—in theory, at least—would read the bar code and transmit the train's location to headquarters. We say "in theory" because the system never worked. Not surprisingly, the bar codes became so covered with dust and grime that they were unreadable. With the satellite system in place, the railroad companies will be able to deliver freight cars with the same precision as overnight carriers delivering packages.

Old rule: Plans get revised periodically
Disruptive technology: High-performance computing
New rule: Plans get revised instantaneously

The sheer capacity of increasingly affordable computing power creates new application possibilities for companies. Take manufacturing, for instance. Today a manufacturer gathers data on product sales, raw materials price and availability, labor supply, and so on and once a month (or once a week) produces a master production schedule. A computer supplied with real-time data from point-of-sale terminals, commodity markets, and perhaps even weather forecasts, among other information sources, could constantly adjust the schedule to match real-time, not historic, needs.

It should be clear from these examples that further advances in technology will break more rules about how we conduct business. Rules that still appear inviolate today may become obsolete in a year or less.

Consequently, exploiting the potential of technologies to change a company's business processes and move it dramatically ahead of its competitors is not a one-time event. Nor is it something a company can do occasionally, say, once a decade. On the contrary, staying on top of new technology and learning how to recognize and incorporate it into an organization must be an ongoing effort—no different from research and development or marketing. It takes a practiced eye and imaginative mind to spot the potential in a technology that does not at first appear to have any obvious application to a company's work or to see past the obvious to the novel applications of a technology that superficially seems useful only for marginally improving the status quo.

Companies need to make technology exploitation one of their core competencies if they are to succeed in a period of ongoing technological change. Those better able to recognize and realize the potentials of new technology will enjoy a continuing and growing advantage over their competitors.

Our view is that if you can buy a technology, it is not new. We subscribe to what might be called the Wayne Gretzky school of technology. Gretzky, who became the National Hockey League's all-time leading scorer at age 28, was once asked what made him a great hockey player. He was exceptional, he answered, "because I go where the puck is *going* to be, not where it *is.*" The same rule applies to technology. Building a strategy around what one can buy in the market today means that a company will always be playing catch up with competitors who have already anticipated it. These competitors know what they are going to do with technology *before* it becomes available, so they will be ready to deploy it when it does become available.

Companies that have had great success with applying technology—American Express, for instance, whose image-processing system allows it to send digitized copies of original receipts to both corporate cardholders and their accounting departments and Chrysler with its satellite communications system for helping dealers manage their parts inventories—were asking for the technology they needed well before it appeared on the market. Year after year, Chrysler sent out requests for proposals (RFPs) that outlined what it wanted; when a vendor eventually responded with the needed capabilities, Chrysler was ready to implement. Management knew what rules they wanted to break with the technology before the technology was even at hand.

Companies cannot see or read about a new technology today and deploy it tomorrow. It takes time to study it, to understand its significance, to conceptualize its potential uses, to sell those uses inside the company, and to plan the deployment. An organization that can execute these preliminaries before the technology actually becomes available will inevitably gain a significant lead on its competition—in many cases, three years or more.

It is entirely possible to stay three years ahead of the market on technology. It takes time to move from laboratory to market; there does not exist a technology that will become important in three years that is not yet demonstrable today. Smart companies can be figuring out how they will use a technology, even while its developers are still polishing their prototypes.

As an essential enabler in reengineering, modern information technology has an importance to the reengineering process that is difficult to overstate. But companies need to beware of thinking that technology is the only essential element in reengineering.

To reengineer a company is to take a journey from the familiar into the unknown. This journey has to begin somewhere and with someone. Where and with whom? That is the question we address in the chapters that follow.

CHAPTER 6

WHO WILL REENGINEER?

Companies don't reengineer processes; people do. Before we delve more deeply into the "what" of the reengineering process, we need to attend to the "who." How companies select and organize the people who actually do the reengineering is key to the success of the endeavor.

We have seen the following roles emerge, either distinctly or in various combinations, during our work with companies that are implementing reengineering.

- *Leader:* a senior executive who authorizes and motivates the overall reengineering effort
- *Process owner:* a manager with responsibility for a specific process and the reengineering effort focused on it
- *Reengineering team:* a group of individuals dedicated to the reengineering of a particular process, who diagnose the existing process and oversee its redesign and implementation
- *Steering committee:* a policy-making body of senior managers who develop the organization's overall reengineering strategy and monitor its progress
- *Reengineering czar:* an individual responsible for developing

reengineering techniques and tools within the company and for achieving synergy across the company's separate reengineering projects

In an ideal world, the relationship among these is as follows: The leader appoints the process owner, who convenes a reengineering team to reengineer the process, with the assistance from the czar and under the auspices of the steering committee. Let's examine these roles and the people who play them in more detail.

Leader

The reengineering leader makes reengineering happen. He or she is a senior executive with enough clout to cause an organization to turn itself inside out and upside down and to persuade people to accept the radical disruptions that reengineering brings. Without a leader, an organization can do some paper studies, can even come up with new process design concepts; but absent a leader, no reengineering will actually happen. Even if it gets started, a leaderless reengineering effort will run out of steam or hit the wall by the time it is ready to implement.

Usually no senior executive is assigned the job of leader. It's a self-nominated and self-appointed role. Someone with the clout to carry it off becomes the leader of reengineering when he or she is seized by a passion to reinvent the company, to make the organization the best in the business, finally to get it completely right.

The leader's primary role is to act as visionary and motivator. By fashioning and articulating a vision of the kind of organization that he or she wants to create, the leader invests everyone in the company with a purpose and a sense of mission. The leader must make clear to everyone that reengineering involves a serious effort that will be seen through to its end. From the leader's convictions and enthusiasm, the organization derives the spiritual energy that it needs to embark on a voyage into the unknown.

The leader also kicks off the organization's reengineering efforts. It is the leader who appoints senior managers as owners of business processes and charges them with achieving breakthroughs in performance. The leader creates the new vision and sets the new standard and, through the owners, induces others to translate that vision into reality.

Leaders must also create an environment conducive to reengineering. Urging people on isn't enough. Any rational person in a corporate environment will react warily, if not cynically, to an executive's insistence that he or she break the rules, defy the received wisdom, and think out of the box. So, while half the leader's job involves urging the process owner and reengineering team to perform, the other half involves supporting them so that they *can* perform. "Be bold," the leader says, "and if you get heat from anyone, pass it on to me. If someone blocks your way, let me know who that person is, and I'll take care of it."

Who fills the leader's role? The role requires someone who has enough authority over all stakeholders in the process(es) that will undergo reengineering to ensure that reengineering *can* happen. This need not be the CEO; in fact, it rarely is. In most large companies, the CEO has concerns that range from raising capital on Wall Street to handling key customers to maintaining peace with the government. Many of these responsibilities direct the CEO's attention outside the company, away from its processes. So, often the role of leader belongs to the chief operating officer or president, whose gaze is directed both outward, toward the customer, and inward, toward the operations of the business.

If a company plans to confine reengineering to just one part of the organization, the leader can occupy a less lofty position. He or she might be the general manager of a division. If that's the case, however, the leader must have authority over the resources involved in performing the division's processes. If, for example, a division uses manufacturing facilities that "belong" to the corporate head of manufacturing, who doesn't report to the division head, then the division head may not have the necessary clout to make changes in manufacturing. So the leader of this reengineering effort would have to reside further up in the hierarchy. For similar reasons, a functional head, such as the vice president of sales or manufacturing, is generally not in a position to play the reengineering leadership role, unless the reengineering effort is completely within the domain of the function.

Leadership isn't just a matter of position, but of character as well. Ambition, restlessness, and intellectual curiosity are the hallmarks of the reengineering leader. A caretaker of the status quo will never be able to muster the passion and enthusiasm the effort requires.

The leader must also *be* a leader. We define a leader not as someone who makes other people do what he or she wants, but as someone who makes them want what he or she wants. A leader doesn't coerce people into change that they resist. A leader articulates a vision and persuades people that they want to become part of it, so that they willingly, even enthusiastically, accept the distress that accompanies its realization.

Moses was a visionary leader. He persuaded the children of Israel that they should go forward toward a land of milk and honey when all they could see around them was sand. One man couldn't force a whole people to set off into the desert; he had to inspire them with his vision. He also set a personal example. When they arrived at the Red Sea, Moses said, "Here's the plan. We're going to march into the sea, the Lord will part the waters, and we'll walk through on dry land." His followers looked at the Red Sea and said to him, "You first." He went, and they followed. Being out front when the risk presents itself is part of leadership. (This story also demonstrates the value of having your boss on your side, as Moses certainly did.)

The reengineering leader can demonstrate leadership through signals, symbols, and systems.

Signals are the explicit messages that the leader sends to the organization about reengineering: what it means, why we are doing it, how we are going about it, and what it will take. Successful reengineering leaders have learned that they always underestimate how much communicating they must do. Giving a speech or two—or ten—doesn't begin to get the message across. Reengineering is a difficult concept for people to assimilate because it cuts against the grain of everything they've done in their careers. In many cases, they also don't see (or they refuse to see) the need for it. Only someone who is serious about reengineering, perhaps to the point of fanaticism, can send the right signals. Winston Churchill defined a fanatic as someone who can't change his mind and won't change the subject. By that definition, fanaticism is needed in a reengineering leader because constant repetition of the reengineering message is essential if people are to understand it and take it seriously.

Symbols are actions that the leader performs to reinforce the content of the signals, to demonstrate that he or she lives by his or her words. Assigning the company's "best and brightest" to reengineering teams, rejecting design proposals that promise only incremental improvement, and removing managers who block the reengineering effort—over and above their intrinsic value—are important symbolic activities. They prove to the organization that the leader is serious about reengineering.

The leader also needs to use management *systems* to reinforce the reengineering message. These systems must measure and reward people's performance in ways that encourage them to attempt major change. Punishing the innovator when an innovation fails is the best way to ensure that no one ever attempts to be innovative. Progressive Insurance, one of the most successful insurance companies in the United States, thrives on constant innovation. Bruce Marlow, the chief operating officer, expresses his company's approach this way: "We never punish failure. We only punish sloppy execution and the failure to recognize reality."

Management systems should reward people who try good ideas that fail, not punish them. At Motorola, the motto is, "We *celebrate* noble failure." An organization that demands constant perfection discourages people from striving and makes them timid. As Voltaire wrote, "The perfect is the enemy of the good."

Some leaders have found it impossible to begin their reengineering efforts in corporate cultures and organizations that would have proved too resistant to change. Ron Compton, for example, CEO of Aetna Life and Casualty, initiated his reengineering program with a set of actions that seemed to have nothing to do with process redesign. He created a new organizational structure that emphasized the autonomy of major business units and eliminated cross subsidies, installed a new senior management team, and carried out a significant reduction in force that slashed costs and signaled the end of Aetna's traditionally paternalistic culture. None of these steps fits our definition of reengineering, but they helped create an environment in which reengineering could succeed. The power of these changes, says Compton, is that they enabled him to tell the organization that he had "burned his bridges." He had dismantled the old Aetna, so the organization could go nowhere but forward. The German phrase *eine Flucht nach Vorn*, a retreat forward, captures the combination of desperation and ambition that many reengineering leaders find necessary to instill in their organizations.

How much of his or her time should the leader devote to reengineering? After all, a senior business manager has other matters to worry about, including keeping the business alive until the results of reengineering begin to show up. We answer this question in two ways. On reengineering per se, the leader need not spend more than a small percentage of his or her time, typically in performing project reviews and making hortatory speeches supporting the reengineering effort. At the same time, reengineering should so suffuse the leader's consciousness and objectives that it underlies everything that he or she does.

Most reengineering failures stem from breakdowns in leadership. Without strong, aggressive, committed, and knowledgeable leadership, there will be no one to persuade the barons running functional silos within the company to subordinate the interests of their functional areas to those of the processes that cross their boundaries. No one will be able to force changes in compensation and measurement systems, no one will be able to compel the human resources organization to redefine its job-rating system. There will be no one to convince the people affected by reengineering that no alternative exists and that the results will be worth the agony of the process.

What if no leader steps forward in the beginning? What if the people first inspired to reengineer aren't positioned high enough in the company's hierarchy to pull it off? Then they must get a leader on board. Doing so will require tact, persistence, and self-effacement. They will have to identify a potential leader, create a sense of urgency in his or her mind, and then introduce the idea of reengineering so that the leader embraces it as his or her own.

We have dwelt on the position of leader because it is so essential to the success of reengineering. Not that the other roles are unimportant, but no other individual involved in reengineering is so key as the leader.

Process Owner

The process owner, who is responsible for reengineering a specific process, should be a senior-level manager, usually with line responsibility, who carries prestige, credibility, and clout within the company. If the leader's job is to make reengineering happen in the large, then the process owner's job is to make it happen in the small, at the individual process level. It is the process owner's reputation, bonus, and career that are on the line when his or her process is undergoing reengineering.

Most companies lack process owners, because in traditional organizations people do not tend to think in process terms. Responsibility for processes is fragmented across organizational boundaries. That's why identifying the company's major processes is a crucial early step in reengineering. (We will have more to say about how this is done in the next chapter.)

After identifying the processes, the leader designates the owners who will guide those processes through reengineering. Process owners are usually individuals who manage one of the functions involved in the process that will undergo reengineering. To do their reengineering jobs, they have to have the respect of their peers and a stomach for reengineering—they must be people who are comfortable with change, tolerant of ambiguity, and serene in adversity.

An owner's job is not to *do* reengineering but to see that it gets done. The owner must assemble a reengineering team and do whatever is required to enable the team to do its job. He or she obtains the resources that the team requires, runs interference with the bureaucracy, and works to gain the cooperation of other managers whose functional groups are involved in the process.

Process owners also motivate, inspire, and advise their teams. They act as the team's critic, spokesperson, monitor, and liaison. When reengineering team members start to produce ideas that make coworkers in the organization unhappy, process owners shield them from the arrows that others will shoot their way. Process owners take the heat so that their teams can concentrate on making reengineering happen.

The process owner's job will not end when the reengineering project is completed. In a process-oriented company, process, not function or geography, will form the basis of organizational structure, so every process will continue to need an owner to attend to its performance.

Reengineering Team

The actual work of reengineering—the heavy lifting—is the job of the reengineering team members. These are the people who must produce the ideas and the plans and who are often then asked to turn them into realities. These are the people who actually reinvent the business.

A small point before we dive into who these people are: No team can reengineer more than one process at a time, which means that a company reengineering more than one process will have more than one reengineering team at work. What we are about to say applies to each of them.

Notice, we call these groups "teams," not committees. To function as a team they should be small—between five and ten people. Each team will have two kinds of people on it, insiders and outsiders.

We define insiders as people who currently work inside the process undergoing reengineering. They come from the various functions involved in the process. They know the process, or at least the parts of it that they encounter in their jobs.

But knowing the existing process and how the company currently performs it is a double-edged sword. Intimate knowledge of the existing process will help the team find its flaws and trace the sources of its performance problems. Proximity to the existing process, however, may hamper thinking about the process in new and imaginative ways.

Insiders sometimes confuse what is with what should be. Consequently, we look for people who have been around long enough to know the ropes but not so long as to think the old process makes sense; they shouldn't have become inured to the illogic of the standard ways of doing things. We also look for mavericks who know the rules but also how to get around them. In general, the insiders assigned to a reengineering team should be the best and the brightest, the company's rising stars.

Next to their knowledge, the most important asset that insiders bring to their reengineering work is their credibility with coworkers. When they say that a new process will work, the people in the organizations from which they've come will believe them. When the time comes to put the new process in place, the insiders will act as key agents in convincing the rest of the organization to buy into the changes.

Insiders by themselves, however, are incapable of reengineering a process. Their individual perspectives may be too narrow, confined to just one part of the process. Further, insiders can hold a vested interest in the existing process and the organization designed to support it. It would be asking too much to expect them, unaided, to overcome their cognitive and institutional biases and to envision radically new ways of working. Left to their own devices, a team made up of insiders will tend to re-create what already exists, with perhaps a 10 percent improvement. They will remain within the frame of the existing process, not break it. To understand what is being changed, the team needs insiders; but to change it, the team needs a disruptive element. These are the outsiders.

Outsiders don't work in the process that's undergoing reengineering, so they bring a higher level of objectivity and a different perspective to the team. Outsiders aren't afraid to ask the emperor about his new clothes; they aren't afraid to ask the naive questions that shatter assumptions and open people's minds to exciting new ways of seeing the world. The outsiders' job on the team is to make waves. Since outsiders are beholden to no one affected by the changes they initiate, they feel more comfortable taking risks.

From where do outsiders come? By definition, they are outside the process, and often, especially in companies that have not reengineered at least once before, they may be from outside the company. Outsiders need to be good listeners and good communicators. They must be big-picture thinkers and quick studies, since they will have to learn a lot in a hurry about each process on which they will work. They need to be imaginative thinkers, capable of envisioning a concept and making it happen.

Companies, in fact, may have many candidates for outsiders inside their organizations. Good places to look are in departments such as engineering, information systems, and marketing, where people with a process orientation and an innovative bent tend to congregate. Companies that don't have appropriate internal outsiders can go outside to find them, typically by engaging consulting firms with track records in reengineering. These consultants bring with them experience that companies may not be able to duplicate on their own.

How many outsiders should serve on the reengineering team? A little contention goes a long way. A ratio of two or three insiders to each outsider is about right.

Insiders and outsiders don't mix easily. As the team members go about their jobs, don't expect sweet reason to rule. Team meetings will more likely resemble sessions of the Russian parliament, which is as it should be. An absence of contention and conflict during reengineering usually signals that nothing productive is happening, but contention and conflict among team members should be directed toward a common end. "Truth," said the Scottish philosopher David Hume, "arises from disagreement amongst friends." To us, friends are people with mutual regard and mutual concern. Team members must be friends who share a common focus: improving the performance of their process. There is no room for private turf and private agendas.

Reengineering teams must be largely self-directed. The process owner is their client, not their boss, and the system that measures and rewards team performance should use as its principal criterion the team's progress toward its target. Moreover, team performance should be the single most important measure of individual member achievement.

To function as a team, members need to work together in one place, which is not as easy as it sounds. It won't happen if the team members remain in the offices they occupied before joining the team. In fact, it won't happen if members stay in offices anywhere. Most companies don't design their facilities with collaborative work in mind. They maintain lots of private or semiprivate rooms designed for solo work and conference rooms for meetings, but they don't have many large spaces suitable for a team to work together in over an extended period of time. This isn't a minor issue; it can prove a serious impediment to a reengineering team's progress. So one job for the leader is to find or commandeer appropriate working space for the team.

Reengineering involves invention and discovery, creativity and synthesis. A reengineering team must feel comfortable with ambiguity. Team members must expect to make mistakes and to learn from them. People not capable of working this way do not belong on the team.

Conventional organizations are analytic and detail-oriented in their problem solving; they place a high premium on finding the right answer the first time. They enshrine what we call the "endless planning, flawless execution" model of problem solving, in which a lengthy period of analysis leads to a plan so perfect that any fool could supposedly carry it out. Reengineering, in contrast, requires the team to go through an iterative learning process as it invents a new way of performing work. Reengineering team members will have to unlearn the traditional problem-solving style, a difficult adjustment for some.

The reengineering team has no official head. Most reengineering teams find it helpful to have a team captain, sometimes appointed by the owner but usually nominated by acclamation by team members. The captain isn't the king, only *primus inter pares*, like George Washington, first among equals. Sometimes an insider and sometimes an outsider, the captain serves as the team's facilitator and quartermaster. His or her job is to enable team members to do their work. The captain may establish the agenda for team meetings, help the team stick to it, and mediate conflicts. Somebody has to attend to the administrative details, such as scheduling and vacation time, and those tasks are likely to fall to the captain as well. However, the captain's primary role is to act as a team member, just like everyone else.

We are often asked three questions about the reengineering team: How much? How long? What next?

When they ask how much, people want to know what percentage of their time team members should expect to devote to the reengineering effort. We are stringent about this requirement. Part-time assignments don't work. A minimum commitment is 75 percent of each team member's time, for insiders and outsiders alike. A lesser obligation will make it extremely difficult to get anything done. It also risks stretching the reengineering effort out so long that it loses momentum and dies. In fact, we strongly urge that organizations assign team members 100 percent to the team. Besides making it easier for the team members to accomplish what they must, a 100 percent commitment sends a powerful signal to the company that management is serious about reengineering.

The reengineering team is not a ninety-day assignment. Members should remain on the team at least through implementation of the first field pilot site, which usually takes a year, but preferably until the reengineering effort is completed. For insiders, then, joining the reengineering team effectively means leaving existing assignments and home organizations, which is as it should be. Team members should sever old ties, so they can be loyal to the process, to the reengineering endeavor, and to one another. They are on the team to represent the company's collective interests, not the parochial interests of their former departments. To reinforce this perspective, insiders should not expect to return to their previous jobs when reengineering is over. Rather, they should expect to become part of the new organization that will perform the new process that they are designing. No incentive is quite so effective as the prospect of having to live with the results of one's work.

So far we have discussed what we call the core reengineering team, the group with direct responsibility for the reengineering effort. This core is usually supplemented with an outer ring of part-time and occasional contributors, who make more narrow and specialized contributions to the effort. Process customers and suppliers are often represented on the outer core to make sure that their perspectives and concerns are heard in a direct, unfiltered way. Specialists with expertise in particular disciplines—such as information technology, human resources, or public relations—are often also included in the outer core. They have information that the team needs, and they can be assigned to carry out particular tasks, such as constructing an information system to support the new process or developing a communications plan to describe the new process to the rest of the organization. These individuals' commitments vary, but they are typically involved on an ad hoc basis.

In addition to the leader and the reengineering team, we typically see two other roles emerge as a company reengineers: steering committee and reengineering czar.

Steering Committee

The reengineering steering committee is an optional aspect of the reengineering governance structure. Some companies swear by it, and others live without it. The steering committee is a collection of senior managers, usually including but not limited to the process owners, who plan the organization's overall reengineering strategy. The leader should chair this group.

Overarching issues that transcend the scope of individual processes and projects get aired in the steering committee. This group decides, for example, the order of priority among all the competing reengineering projects and how resources should be allocated. Process owners and their teams come to the steering committee for help when they run into problems that they can't resolve on their own. Committee members hear and resolve conflicts among process owners. Part Supreme Court, part mutual aid society, part House of Lords, the steering committee can do much to help an extensive reengineering program succeed.

Reengineering Czar

Process owners and their teams focus on their specific reengineering projects. Who then is concerned with actively managing the reengineering effort as a whole, the aggregate of reengineering efforts across the whole organization? The leader has the right perspective but lacks the time for day-to-day management of the reengineering effort, so he or she requires strong staff support. We call this role the reengineering czar.

The reengineering czar serves as the leader's chief of staff for reengineering. In principle, he or she should report directly to the leader, but we have seen almost every imaginable reporting variation.

The czar has two main functions: one, enabling and supporting each individual process owner and reengineering team; and, two, coordinating all ongoing reengineering activities.

A newly appointed process owner's first call should be to the czar, who knows what needs to get done to make reengineering happen. As keeper of the company's reengineering techniques, the czar should have approaches for accomplishing reengineering that he or she can explain to process owners who are new to the task.

The czar can help select the insiders for the team and can identify—or even provide—appropriate outsiders. The czar will also advise new owners on the issues and problems they are likely to encounter. The czar has been down the reengineering road before, so new travelers won't find it lonesome and frightening.

The czar also keeps a watchful eye on process owners to keep them on track as they proceed through reengineering. The czar may convene and moderate some discussions among the process owners. When the owners of the order fulfillment and material acquisition processes need to coordinate their efforts, the czar should make sure that they do.

The reengineering czar is also concerned with developing the infrastructure for reengineering so that not every reengineering project seems like the first one the company has ever done. Field-tested techniques and a stable of experienced outsiders are two ways in which companies can benefit from their own previous experiences. But there is also a third.

Some elements of an organization's infrastructure, if put in place before the implementation phase of a reengineering project, can smooth and speed the implementation. One such element is information technology. Often, it is possible to anticipate early in a reengineering project (or even before it gets underway) what kind of information systems the organization will need to support the reengineered process. Installing the hardware and supporting software—the platforms—for these systems early will make implementation go much faster. Similarly, if companies learn from early reengineering efforts that reengineered processes demand people who exist only in small numbers in the organization, the company can then recruit more of these people before subsequent reengineering efforts start demanding them, saving time and anguish for the managers of these later projects. There is also much to anticipate in terms of changes in management systems regarding workers' compensation, rewards, and performance measurements. Part of the czar's job is to anticipate these infrastructure needs and to meet them even before they arise.

One final point on the subject of the reengineering czar: We have seen instances when the czar becomes a problem by becoming too controlling and forgetting that the leader and the process owner are in charge. Organizations must guard against this possibility and always remember that the work of reengineering has to be the line manager's job.

These, then, are the toilers in the vineyard of reengineering: the leader, the process owner, the team with its insiders and outsiders, the steering committee, and the czar. In some companies they may have other names or the reengineering roles may be defined differently. That's okay. Reengineering is a young art, and there is room for more than one approach.

From the issue of who reengineers we now turn to the next question: What gets reengineered?

CHAPTER 7

THE HUNT FOR REENGINEERING OPPORTUNITIES

Processes, not organizations, are the object of reengineering. Companies don't reengineer their sales or manufacturing departments; they reengineer the work that the people in those departments do.

The confusion between organizational units and processes as objects of reengineering arises because departments, divisions, and groups are familiar to people in business, while processes are not; organizational lines are visible, plainly drawn on organization charts, and processes are not; organizational units have names, and processes most often do not.

This chapter illustrates how companies identify their business processes, suggests techniques for selecting the processes that should be reengineered and the order of their reengineering, and stresses the importance of understanding specific processes before attempting to redesign them.

Processes are not something that we invented in order to write about them. Every company on earth consists of processes. Processes are what companies do.

Processes in a company correspond to natural business activities, but they are often fragmented and obscured by the organizational structures. Processes are invisible and unnamed because people think about the individual departments, not about the process with which all of them are involved. Processes also tend to be unmanaged in that people are put in charge of the departments or work units, but no one is given the responsibility for getting the whole job—the process—done.

One way to get a better handle on the processes that make up a business is to give them names that express their beginning and end states. These names should imply all the work that gets done between their start and finish. Manufacturing, which sounds like a department name, is better called the procurement-to-shipment process. Some other recurring processes and their state-change names:

- Product development: concept to prototype
- Sales: prospect to order
- Order fulfillment: order to payment
- Service: inquiry to resolution

Just as companies have organization charts, they can have process maps that give a picture of how work flows through the company. A process map also creates a vocabulary to help people discuss reengineering.

This can be seen in the high-level process map (slightly simplified) of Texas Instruments' semiconductor business. Four especially interesting characteristics of TI's process map stand out.

The first is its simplicity as compared to an organization chart of the same company. The process map shows only six processes for a $4 billion business. "You know," commented a TI executive about this map, "until we drew this picture we thought we were a lot more complicated than we really are." TI is not unusual in this respect; hardly any company contains more than ten or so principal processes.

TI Semiconductor Business Process Map

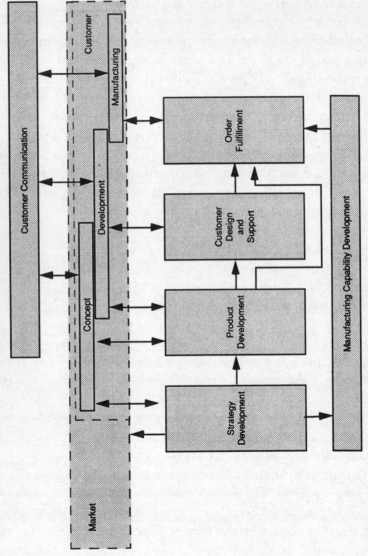

At TI's semiconductor division, the main business processes are strategy development, product development, customer design and support, manufacturing capability development, customer communications, and order fulfillment. Each of these processes converts inputs into outputs.

The *strategy development* process converts market requirements into a business strategy, which identifies markets to be served and products and services to be offered. The *product development* process uses this output as input in order to produce new product designs. In some of TI's business lines, general product designs have to be customized for particular customers. The *customer design and support* process creates these so-called qualified designs as its outputs, using standard product designs and customer requirements as inputs.

The TI process map shows three other high-level processes. Two of them have names that are probably unfamiliar: *manufacturing capability development* and *customer communications*. The manufacturing capability development process takes a strategy as its input and produces a factory as its output. Customer communications inputs are customer questions and inquiries; its outputs are heightened interest in TI products and consolidated responses to customers.

Order fulfillment is the company's payoff. Order fulfillment converts an order request, a product design, and a factory into a product that is delivered into a customer's hands.

The process map displays a clear and comprehensive picture of the work at Texas Instruments' semiconductor division: Strategy development creates a strategy; product development generates an overall product design; customer design and support produces a custom design; manufacturing capability produces a plant; customer communications answers customer questions and inquiries; order fulfillment delivers what the customer wants.

The second important point to be made about TI's process map is that it includes something that is almost never displayed on a company's organization chart: the customer. On the process map, TI's customer is right in the center.

Point number three is that the TI process map also includes noncustomers in its view of processes. These noncustomers, who are all potential customers, are included within the "market" label on the map. These noncustomers provide important input to the strategy development process.

Fourth, the process map reflects TI's recognition that its customers are companies with processes too. The customer is not seen as a monolith, but in terms of three key processes with which TI interacts: concept formulation, product development, and manufacturing. This perspective indicates that TI appreciates how its customers' business works and how it can contribute to that work and the customers' processes.

A few processes one might expect to find are not on the map—manufacturing, for instance. Texas Instruments is a chip maker, but the process portrait does not depict manufacturing as one of its main processes. Instead, manufacturing is a subprocess of order fulfillment—just one of the subprocesses that must get done to deliver a chip to the customer. Sales doesn't show up in the picture, either. Sales is not a process, but a department—a collection of people. Salespeople, however, are involved in many of the processes. They're involved in order fulfillment because another subprocess of order fulfillment is order acquisition, which is primarily performed by salespeople. Salespeople will also be involved in the customer communication and in product development processes.

Clearly, then, this map does not represent everything that happens at TI. It shows only the high-level processes. But each of these can explode into various subprocesses—usually numbering no more than half a dozen or so—on separate subprocess maps. Together, the process and subprocesses maps give a simple but effective picture of what TI—or any company—does.

Process maps don't require months of work to construct; several weeks is the norm. But this task does induce headaches, because it requires people to think across the organizational grain. It's not a picture of the organization, which is what people are used to seeing and drawing, but a depiction of the work that is being done. When it's finished, the process map should not surprise anyone. In fact, people may wonder why drawing it took as long as it did, since the finished map will be so easy to understand, even obvious. "Of course," people should say, "that's just a model of what we do around here."

Choosing the Processes to Reengineer

Once processes are identified and mapped, deciding which ones require reengineering and the order in which they should be tackled is not a trivial part of the reengineering effort. No company can reengineer all its high-level processes simultaneously. Typically, organizations use three criteria to help them make their choices. The first is dysfunction: Which processes are in the deepest trouble? The second is importance: Which processes have the greatest impact on the company's customers? The third is feasibility: Which of the company's processes are at the moment most susceptible to successful redesign?

In looking for dysfunction, the most obvious processes to consider are those that a company's executives already know are in trouble: *broken processes*. As a rule, people are clear about which processes in their companies need reengineering. The evidence is everywhere and generally hard to miss.

A product development process that hasn't hatched a new product in five years can safely be said to be broken. If employees spend time typing data from a computer printout into a computer terminal or from one terminal into another, whatever process they're working on is probably broken. If people's work cubicle walls and their computer screens are papered with Post-it notes reminding them to fix this or look into that, the processes in which they're involved are probably broken too.

Let's look behind some of these symptoms of process distress or dysfunction to the diseases that usually cause them.

Symptom: Extensive information exchange, data redundancy, and rekeying

Disease: Arbitrary fragmentation of a natural process

When employees are keying data taken from one computer into another, it is a symptom of what we call "terminal disease." The efficiency-minded manager's typical response to a case of terminal disease is to look for a way to rekey the material more quickly or, if the manager is more technologically oriented, to find a way to link the terminals so the material can travel electronically from one system to another. Both solutions treat the symptom, not the disease.

When the same information travels back and forth among different organizational groups—whether it's rekeyed each time or transmitted electronically—it suggests that a natural activity has been fragmented. Well-designed natural organizational units should send finished products to one another. Extensive communications is a way of coping with unnatural boundaries. The way to fix the problem is to put the pieces of that activity or process back together. Another name for doing that is *cross-functional integration*, which allows organizations to capture data just one time and then share it, instead of finding faster ways to ship it back and forth.

Terminal disease doesn't involve only computerized data. If people in different parts of the organization have to telephone one another frequently or send a lot of memos or e-mail messages, that probably means a natural process has been inappropriately broken apart. The typical response to this form of terminal disease is to give the people affected by it more communications links—another phone line, a fancier fax, and so forth. But that treats the symptom, not the disease. Indeed, the new devices often fail to treat even the symptom. Our version of Parkinson's law says that "work expands to fill the amount of *equipment* available for its completion." Give people more communications capacity and they will communicate more and still feel it's not enough.

The fact is, although collaboration may be necessary for some processes, people should not be calling one another *more:* they should be calling one another *less*. To treat the disease, we have to find out why two people need to call one another so often. If what they do is so closely linked, maybe it should be done by one person—a case worker—or by a case team.

Good organizational boundaries should be relatively opaque. In other words, what goes on inside one organizational unit should not be seen or matter very much to people outside it. Organizations should have a thin pipeline connecting them to the rest of the world. If the boundaries of two or more organizations have to be transparent to one another, they probably ought not to be different organizations in the first place.

Symptom: Inventory, buffers, and other assets
Disease: System slack to cope with uncertainty

Many companies are moving to JIT—just-in-time inventory; their current reality in most cases is JIC—just-in-case inventory. Companies and organizations within companies know that they will have to supply their output to customers, internal or external. Usually, they're just not certain when the demand will come or how much the customer will need. So they always squirrel just a little extra away somewhere (and sometimes they squirrel away a lot). We are not just referring to physical assets, either. People create little buffer caches of work, information, cash, and even extra workers against unexpected demand.

The conventional reaction to JIC inventory is to create better inventory management tools. What a company really should work on is getting rid of the inventory. It is there only to take up the slack introduced into the system by uncertainty. Remove the uncertainty, and we have no slack to worry about, so we won't need the inventory.

One way to rid an organization of uncertainty is by structuring processes so that suppliers and customers plan and schedule their respective work together.

Symptom: High ratio of checking and control to value adding
    work
Disease: Fragmentation

A lot of work goes on in organizations that does not add value to the company's product or service. We have a simple test for distinguishing work that adds value from work that does not. Take the customer's perspective and ask, "Do I care?" If the answer is no, the work adds no value. Does the customer care about a company's internal controls, audits, management, and reporting? Absolutely not. That sort of checking and control work doesn't benefit the customer, only the company. It does not contribute to the value of the product or the service.

As long as companies consist of people, some amount of checking and control will be unavoidable. The issue is not whether non-value-adding work exists in an organization, but whether it forms too great a portion of all the work the organization performs.

Checking and control work is, of course, a symptom, not the disease. The root cause—the reason executives and managers think they must perform checking and control work—is the incompetence and mistrust that can come from fragmentation. The objective in reengineering is not to make checking and control more efficient, but to eliminate its root causes.

Symptom: Rework and iteration
Disease: Inadequate feedback along chains

Rework and iteration both involve doing work again that has

been done once—repainting a part that was painted the wrong color or writing a document several times over. Most often rework and iteration are the consequence of inadequate feedback in a long work process. Problems are caught not when they happen but only much later in the process, requiring more than one step to be redone.

The objective in reengineering is not to get the rework done more efficiently, but to eliminate it entirely by doing away with the mistakes and confusion that necessitate it.

Symptom: Complexity, exceptions, and special cases
Disease: Accretion onto a simple base

When most processes begin life, they are usually quite simple. But they grow complex over time, since every time a new wrinkle or contingency develops, someone modifies the process by adding a special case or a rule to deal with exceptions. Soon the simple process is buried under exceptions and special cases. We may then struggle to simplify what has become unbelievably complicated, but we will fail.

In reengineering we uncover and restore the original, clean process, then create other processes for the other situations. That means we end up with two or more processes instead of just one.

Organizations have become accustomed to standardizing, which means trying to satisfy every contingency with a single process. They create one standard—and complicated—process that has decision points along its entire length. We now know that in process design it is better to install a decision point up front that can send work along one of several simple processes.

The examples listed identify a set of common symptoms, or dysfunctions that we often encounter in companies and the diseases, or process problems, to which they are usually connected. But as we continue to stress, reengineering is as much an art as it is a science, and symptoms don't always point organizational physicians to the correct diagnosis. Sometimes the symptoms can be seriously misleading. In one organization with which we've worked, the order fulfillment processes were badly flawed, but the company's customers didn't think that was the case; they thought the order fulfillment process was superb. They received exactly what they ordered when they wanted it. Superficially, the process appeared healthy. Where did the problem lie? It turned out that the company's sales were limping badly. Was the sales process broken? No. Rather, the order fulfillment process was in such bad condition that customers received their products on time only because salespeople went to the warehouse, picked up the orders, and delivered them themselves. That pleased the customers, but salespeople were making deliveries instead of selling.

In such a situation, we call the slipping sales a secondary sign of dysfunction; a process is broken over here, but the symptoms show up over there. Many times the evidence that a process isn't working exists but it appears somewhere other than in the obvious places. So, while data may indicate that something is broken, it may not indicate accurately which process isn't working well.

Importance, or impact on outside customers, is the second criterion to consider when deciding which of the company's processes to reengineer and in what order. Even processes that deliver their outputs to customers inside the company may be of major importance and value to outside customers. However, companies can't simply ask their customers directly which processes are most important to them, because customers, even if they are familiar with the process terminology, have no reason to know in much detail the processes their suppliers use.

Customers are a good source of information in comparing the relative importance of various processes, however. Companies can determine what issues their customers care strongly about—issues such as product cost, on-time delivery, product features, and so on. These issues can then be correlated with the processes that most influence them as an aid to creating a priority list of those processes that need reconstruction.

The third criterion, *feasibility*, entails considering a set of factors that determine the likelihood that a particular reengineering effort will succeed. One of these factors is scope. Generally, the larger a process—the more organizational units it involves—the broader its scope. A greater payoff is possible when a process larger in scope is reengineered, but the likelihood of its success will be lower. Broad scope means orchestrating more constituencies, affecting more organizations, and involving more managers who have their own agendas.

Similarly, high cost reduces feasibility. A reengineering effort that requires major investment in an information-processing system, for example, will encounter more hurdles than one that does not.

The strength of the reengineering team and the commitment of the process owner are also factors to be considered in assessing the feasibility of reengineering a particular process.

We must emphasize that the method used to decide among reengineering opportunities is not a formal one. The three criteria we have outlined—dysfunction, impact, and feasibility—must be used with wisdom to help make choices.

Management might also ask whether a particular business process has a significant effect on the company's strategic direction. Does it have a high impact on customer satisfaction? Is the company's performance in this process far below the best-in-class standard? Is it unable to gain more from this process without reengineering? Is this process antiquated? The more yeses to questions such as these, the stronger the argument for reengineering that process. No two organizations will weigh all of those questions equally. They are, however, the kinds of questions that managers should raise in their search for reengineering opportunities.

Understanding Processes

Once a process has been selected for reengineering, a process owner designated, and a team convened, the next step is not redesign—not yet. The next step is to "understand" the current process.

Before a reengineering team can proceed to redesign, it needs to know some things about the existing process: what it does, how well (or poorly) it performs, and the critical issues that govern its performance. Since the team's goal is not to improve the existing process, it does not need to analyze and document the process to expose all of its details. Rather, the team members require a high-level view, just enough so that they have the intuition and insight necessary to create a totally new and superior design.

Nonetheless, one of the most frequently committed errors in reengineering is that at this stage reengineering teams try to analyze a process in agonizing detail rather than attempt to understand it. People are prone to analyze because it is a familiar activity. We know how to do it. It also feels good, because analysis gives us an illusion of progress. We come to the office every morning, and we have calls to make, interviews to perform, data to graph. We produce lots of paper, and it all feels comfortable and satisfying. But analysis doesn't necessarily move us any closer to real understanding.

Detailed process analysis of a conventional sort may be useful to help persuade others in the organization that reengineering is necessary or desirable, but that task is part of change management. What the team is now looking for is knowledge and insight. Because the team doesn't have to collect and analyze volumes of quantitative data, understanding a process is less complex and time-consuming than analyzing it. However, it is no less difficult. In some ways, understanding is harder than analysis.

Traditional process analysis takes the process inputs and outputs as given and looks purely *inside* the process to measure and examine what goes on. Process understanding, in contrast, takes nothing for granted. A reengineering team attempting to *understand* a process does not accept the existing output as a given. Part of understanding a process is comprehending what the process's customer does with that output.

The best place for the reengineering team to begin to understand a process is on the customer end. What are the customers' real requirements? What do they say they want and what do they really need, if the two are different? What problems do they have? What processes do they perform with the output? Since the eventual goal of redesigning a process is to create one that better meets customer needs, it is critical that the team truly understands these needs. Understanding customer needs doesn't mean asking customers what those needs are. They'll say only what they think they want.

For example, in the case we discussed earlier involving Wal-Mart and Procter & Gamble, P&G might simply have asked Wal-Mart, "What would you like our invoices to look like?" or "Do you want the goods delivered faster?" But that is not what happened.

Instead, P&G and Wal-Mart together stepped back and asked, "What is Wal-Mart's real challenge?" The answer in this case was maximizing its profits from selling diapers. Then P&G could ask, "How can we help you sell diapers more profitably? What problems do you have? What do you need?" This is very different from, "How can we help you improve the quality of the existing interaction between us?" Understanding means considering the customer's underlying goals and problems, not just the mechanics of the process that links the two organizations together.

This understanding cannot be obtained merely by asking customers what they want, since they will tend to answer from their own unexpanded mindset. They'll say they want it—whatever "it" they already get—a little faster, a little better, a little less expensively. Customers, when asked, will respond with not very surprising ideas for making incremental improvements to the existing process. That is not what a reengineering team is after.

Rather, a reengineering team has to understand the customers better than they understand themselves. Toward that end, the team, or some of its members, might move in and observe or actually work with customers in their own environments. Doing this is another way in which gaining understanding differs from analysis. In traditional analysis, people collect information through interviews that take place in offices or conference rooms. They don't interview at real work sites, because it is considered much too noisy and distracting there. So analysts take people out of their work environment, sit them down, and ask them to explain what they do. What people tell analysts, however, is what they *think* they should be doing, what they happen to remember, or what they've been told to say; they do *not* say what they actually do. What people do and what they say they do are almost never the same.

A better way to acquire information about what customers do is to watch them do it. A still better way is for team members to do it themselves. Neither observation nor participation will make experts out of team members after a few days or weeks, but they will come away from the experience with a better idea of what is important and what is not than they would from any interview.

Being there, not just hearing about being there, can help team members see beyond the customers' blinders as well as their own biases. The point is not to learn how to do the customers' work but to understand their business—and to gather ideas.

Ideas will spring from team members seeing and comprehending how the customer uses the output of the process. If, for example, the customer has to partially disassemble the output before using it, maybe the output should be shipped in a partially assembled state. The team is looking for ideas about ways the process can better serve the customer.

Once the team understands what the process customer might need, the next step is to figure out what the process currently provides—to understand the current process itself.

The goal is to understand the what and the why, not the how, of the process, because in redesign the team is less concerned with how the process works today than in what the new process will have to do. Knowing what and why, the team can begin its redesign with a blank sheet of paper. To learn the what and why, the reengineering team can take almost all of what we have just said about observing and participating in customers' work and apply those same remarks to the process itself. Observing and performing the process is the best way to develop insight into it. However, the team must be vigilant about avoiding the temptation to overstudy. The goal must be to move quickly to redesign.

Before concluding we should comment on another tool that is available to reengineering teams, namely benchmarking. Essentially, benchmarking means looking for the companies that are doing something best and learning how they do it in order to emulate them.

The problem with benchmarking is it can restrict the reengineering team's thinking to the framework of what is already being done in its company's own industry. By aspiring only to be as good as the best in its industry, the team sets a cap on its own ambitions. Used this way, benchmarking is just a tool for catching up, not for jumping way ahead.

Benchmarking can, however, spark ideas in the team—especially if teams use as their benchmarks companies from outside their own industries. For example, the idea around which Hewlett-Packard reengineered its materials purchasing process came from a senior manager who joined the company from the automotive industry. He brought with him a completely different mindset—and a new purchasing model.

If a team is going to benchmark, it should benchmark from the best in the world, not the best in its industry. If a team's company is in the consumer packaged-goods business, the question is not who is the product developer in packaged goods, but who is the best product developer—period. That's the company from which the team might get great ideas.

There's an old story that when Xerox decided to improve its order fulfillment process, it didn't compare itself to other copier companies, but to the mail-order clothing retailer, L.L. Bean.

There's still a danger, however, even in using benchmarking to generate new ideas. What if it doesn't turn up a new idea? It is possible that no one in another company has had a great idea yet that is applicable to the process that the team is seeking to reengineer. Just because that's the case, however, doesn't give the reengineering team an excuse to be complacent. Rather, team members might consider it a challenge: *They* can create the new, world-class benchmark.

Keep in mind that by diagnosing the company's current processes, the reengineering team is learning a great deal about them, but not so that it can fix them. Old processes can take only so much fixing before the marginal benefits aren't worth the bother. Besides, reengineering teams don't look for marginal benefits, but order-of-magnitude improvements. Just fixing the old processes is not enough.

Instead, the team is trying to study the existing processes so it can learn and understand what is critical in their performance. The more team members know about the real objectives of a process, the better they will be at its redesign.

CHAPTER 8

THE EXPERIENCE OF PROCESS REDESIGN

For a writer, nothing is so exciting and at the same time so terrifying as a clean sheet of paper or a blank computer screen. For a reengineering team, it's the first redesign session. All the team has to do in this session is to get a start on reenvisioning the company and inventing a new way of doing its work.

Redesign is the most nakedly creative part of the entire reengineering process. More than any other, it demands imagination, inductive thinking, and a touch of craziness. In redesigning processes, the reengineering team abandons the familiar and seeks the outrageous. Redesign asks the team members, especially the insiders, to suspend their belief in the rules, procedures, and values that they've honored their whole working lives. Redesign is unnerving precisely because the team can do whatever it likes.

The bad news about redesigning a work process is that it is not algorithmic and routine. There are no ten-step procedures that will mechanically produce a radical new process design.

The good news about redesign is that while it may require creativity, it's not necessary to start with an entirely blank slate. Enough companies have now done reengineering for us to be able to discern some recurring patterns in the processes they have redesigned. Techniques that have proved effective for some companies will work for others—or at least pieces of them will. So even though no hard and fast rules yet exist for process redesign, we do know the principles on which redesign depends, and we now have some precedents.

Almost anyone who has been through business school or who has a few years of corporate management experience can design a traditional business process, because well-established guidelines exist for doing that. For instance, we know almost intuitively that in a traditional process work should be broken into simple tasks; we know the limits of a manager's span of control; we know about economies of scale and the need for control, accountability, and budgeting. Given a business activity—paying vendors for received materials, for instance—almost anyone who has been around a business could design a traditional process for accomplishing it.

It turns out that nontraditional processes also contain recurring characteristics and themes. Not many people know what these are yet, but they are reflections of the principles of reengineering that we have been discussing throughout this book.

Some day the characteristics of reengineered business processes will undoubtedly be as obvious and as well known as the traditional business processes are today. The reason that these nontraditional characteristics and themes are not intuitively obvious to most people today is that they are still new. They have not yet become part of the collective conventional wisdom.

So how does a reengineering team proceed with its redesign effort? It's the first morning of the redesign phase. The team members are in their meeting room, the coffee is fresh, and the chalkboard is blank. Where to begin?

Process redesign should be breathtaking on account of its potential effects on the company, but it needn't be intimidating. We've developed some techniques that teams can use to get themselves started, and we have some ideas about how to keep people's creative juices flowing during redesign.

In this chapter, we're going to handle redesign in two ways. First, we'll take readers through a short scenario that illustrates how the first day of a redesign session might go. Our objective here is to give people a feel for the redesign process and to show that it need not be mysterious or daunting. Then we'll introduce and illustrate some of the techniques and devices that reengineering teams have found to be useful aids in process redesign.

The scene is a meeting of the reengineering team at Imperial Insurance, a fictitious but representative auto insurance company. The team's charter is to redesign the accident claims process for Imperial, whose claims payout has soared in recent years. Imagine that this is the team's first redesign session and that you are an outsider sitting in. All you know about the insurance business is what the average person knows and a few things that the team captain covers before the redesign session begins.

First, the captain says, Imperial believes that it is paying out more than it should in settling auto accident claims. The claims typically involve two kinds of payments—one covering injury to people and the other covering damage to automobiles. Settlements on both kinds of claims are rising rapidly.

With medical costs in general growing more expensive, it is not surprising, the leader says, that medical claims settlements are becoming costlier, but the increase in auto damage claims, on the other hand, is a paradox. Some years ago, consumers began buying policies with higher collision deductibles, and the assumption in the industry then was that collision damage claims would go down. But they didn't. They went up. Customers, it now seems, buy the higher deductible policies to cut their premium costs, but after an accident they try to get the company to pay the full cost of repair anyhow. They persuade the body shop to make its estimate high enough to cover the actual repair cost plus some or all of the deductible.

Second, the captain says, Imperial has internal cost problems too. For every $7 it pays out to settle a claim, the company spends $1 just to process the claim. Furthermore, the company requires an average of forty days to settle a claim, and that's if the claimant doesn't choose to litigate.

He then describes, in a nutshell, Imperial's claims settlement process. When an accident occurs, the claimant first calls his or her agent, who then notifies the company. It can take three days for the company to receive notification by phone, mail, or in person; to enter the notification into the computer; and to get a representative assigned who is qualified to handle the claim.

Once a rep is assigned to the case, his or her first task is to verify that the claimant's policy was current at the time of the accident. If not, the process ends there. If the policy was current, the process continues.

The next series of tasks boils down to getting answers to two basic questions. Whose insurance company is going to pay, and what is it going to cost to settle this claim?

To ascertain costs, the rep discusses the injuries and their treatment with doctors and the injured parties and sets up an appraisal to estimate the cost of repair to the cars. A lot of telephone work is involved here.

To determine who is at fault, the rep schedules interviews with the insured, any other claimants, witnesses, and the police; the rep will also probably make multiple visits to these people and to the accident scene.

Many variables affect the determination of both the repair and the medical costs: How much fixing do the cars really need? Do we have to use factory-made replacement parts or can we use after-market parts? How much medical treatment is enough medical treatment?

None of these questions is easily answered, and it typically takes a rep thirty-five days from the time of the accident to gather enough information to decide whether to offer the claimants a settlement and, if so, to decide how much to offer.

If everyone accepts the settlement offered, the process ends, having stretched out, on average, more than forty days. If any claimant decides to litigate, however, the process can drag on forever. It is not uncommon for litigation to take five years.

For all claims against it, Imperial's average settlement, according to the team captain, comes to $3,500. The internal cost of reaching that settlement runs, on average, $500.

And that's about all you and the team know about Imperial's claims settlement process (which is typical for the industry). The reengineering team's assignment is to redesign the process so that Imperial's auto insurance business becomes profitable. Team members look at one another and the blank yellow pads in front of them. Where to begin?

"Separate those with bodily injury from those without," suggests a team member. "Our biggest exposure comes when there's bodily injury."

"So why not triage by exposure?" says your neighbor. "Large exposure, small exposure. Sometimes, there can be little or no bodily injury but lots of potential property damage."

"Okay," says the team captain, "we could triage by exposure—small and large. Small exposure would be what? Let's say, no bodily injury and minor damage. Large exposure would be everything else. If we did that, then what? How do we handle the two kinds of claims differently?"

"Well," says a woman across the table, "right now, with overhead and so on it costs us about as much per hour to work on a small claim as on a large one, so I'd say we should try to get the small ones settled fast. They're not worth spending much time on."

"What if we didn't handle them at all?" asks a man at the end of the table. "What if we just paid them, whatever they were, so long as they were smaller than some amount?"

"I don't know," says the captain. "What if we did do that?"

"We have to do *something*," says the woman across from you.

"Let the agent do it," says the man at the end. "If the claim is less than some amount, just let the agent handle it. The agent can pay it.

That way it gets done fast, the agent cements his or her client relationship, and we don't invest any time at all in it."

The captain is taking notes on the chalkboard when the man on your left pipes up: "Let the body shop handle it."

Everyone looks at him. Body shops are not traditionally the insurance company's friend.

"How interesting," the captain finally responds after a few seconds' pause. "Let the body shop handle it."

"Yeah," the man says. "They're the ones that determine the price of repair anyway. Maybe there's a way to get them working *for* us instead of being in cahoots with clients that are trying to rip us off."

A crazy idea? Maybe not. Currently when auto body damage is involved, Imperial sends out an appraiser who looks at the cars and determines an appropriate cost of repair. Meanwhile, the customer is getting his or her own estimates, so the company often ends up arguing with its client over the cost of repair. Who is happy in the end? Usually no one.

A man from the sales side of the business says he doesn't think the idea is crazy. "What do we give the customer now?" he asks. "A check. But what does the customer really want? A repaired car. What if we could triage these claims, and if there was no bodily injury and only minor damage, then we tell the client, just take the car to this auto body shop and they'll take care of it—or, better, tell the customer, here's a list of approved body shops. Pick the one most convenient to you, and they'll take care of it."

Naturally, someone asks what he'd do about fraud—body shops that pad their bills or customers who make claims for accidents that never occurred—and a long discussion follows. The gist of the idea that emerges is this: First, the company could designate preferred-provider body shops that would value the steady business and want to keep it. They would cooperate with Imperial in periodic statistical monitoring of the pricing and the quality of their repairs. As for the dishonest customer, Imperial could make claim frequency part of the triage process.

"So," the captain sums up, "here's an idea that we think might work. We set up a triage system. We get a claim for an accident involving no bodily injury and only moderate damage. It comes from a customer who hasn't made a claim in ten years. We can therefore assume that it's not fraud. There's no large exposure. And we are pretty sure the body shop isn't going to rip us off, because we'll be running a statistical audit. So we send the customer a list of approved body shops and pay the bill when it comes in. That's pretty straightforward, it cuts out a lot of administrative expense, and we can get the claim settled in a lot less time."

He writes on the chalkboard for a minute and then asks the group whether there isn't something more they could do with this notion—settling claims fast.

In traditional insurance claims processes, time has always been considered important. Most claims operations tended to think the *slower* they paid the better, because the company could hold on to the money longer and collect more investment income on it.

"Why might we want to speed it up?" the captain asks and looks around at the group. There's a man sitting next to you on the other side who hasn't said anything yet.

"I'll tell you why," he says, "because it might help keep the client away from personal-injury lawyers." In the auto insurance industry as a whole, statistics show that when an attorney is involved the payout to the customer is many times greater than when there is no attorney.

"When are customers most likely to call an attorney?" the man asks rhetorically. "Right at the beginning. You're in an auto accident. You call your agent. You're stressed, angry, unhappy. The agent takes down a lot of information, and then what happens? Nothing, not a damn thing. We spend the next week or so passing paper back and forth, and as far as the claimant is concerned, no one is doing anything for her or him. No wonder they start calling their lawyers."

"What actually happens during those first few days," the captain reminded the rest of the team, "is that reports sit around in in-baskets. We have to find the right rep, who may be on vacation or on the road with another case. Something is happening, but not so the client notices, and we also incur extra claims costs as a result. So if we want to speed this process up, what should we do?"

Someone suggests an 800 number, well publicized, that customers could call. Someone suggests having accident investigation teams in the office, on call, twenty-four hours a day. Someone suggests giving clients cellular phones so they could call from their cars. Someone suggests installing alarms in car airbags that would call the company automatically if the air bag deployed in an accident. Someone suggests tying in to the police communication system for reporting accidents.

"Good, good, good," the captain says, taking notes on the board. "The idea here is to get rapid notification of the accident. Let's review what we have from the beginning. Through one mechanism or another we compress the time required to start the claims process. We get early notification. We check the coverage, we get some basic data about the event, and then we do triage. Easy case? Let the agent pay it off or send the car to one of our preferred-provider body shops to take care of it. What about the other cases, though, the ones we can't get rid of quickly? Are there some rules that need to be broken here? Anybody?"

"I don't know much about insurance," you say (the first time you've spoken up in this redesign meeting), "but from what I've heard there seems to be a rule that I think needs to be broken. It's the one that says that the company won't do much for the claimant until it decides who's at fault. From a customer's point of view, I think the rule ought to be, fix it first and decide whose fault it is later."

"That's a good statement of a rule that could be broken," the captain tells you. "What if we just eliminated the rule? Maybe we don't need a rule about what we do first. We go to work right away on both fronts—getting things fixed and finding fault. We don't wait to pay until we've found fault."

"Wait, wait," cries another reengineering team member, who has problems with the idea of paying out money that the company might not owe. Another long discussion ensues. The group decides that the company might easily pay money that it didn't owe, but in most cases it would recover that amount from the other insurance company. Plus, its total payout would still be smaller, people feel, if speedy action reduces the number of lawsuits filed against it.

"What else do we need to do here?" the captain asks. "What's the problem from the claimant's point of view? Our visitor (you) raised this point."

"No contact," someone responds.

"Meaning what?"

"We may be working, but the claimant still thinks nothing is going on."

"Suppose you're a claimant," the captain suggests. "You're in the hospital. Your back hurts. You don't know about your car. How do you feel? Terrible. What should we do?"

"Send someone to hold your hand," a team member says.

"Right," says another. "More generally, we've got to get away from the idea that our whole role is to issue a check. Our goal has to change. Instead of issuing checks it should be keeping claimants happy."

"How do we do that?" the captain asks.

"Solve their problems," the last man says.

"How?"

Lots of talk ensues now about what the claimants' problems are and how they get solved. What the company does currently, for instance, is allow clients whose cars are wrecked to rent replacements pending repairs. But, the group decides, that's not solving the customer's problem. That's letting the customer solve his or her own problem, with us just paying for it afterward. Anyway, it's expensive. The claimant pays retail for a rental car. We could strike a better deal with the rental agency.

At this point, the team decides to give the claimants names to make discussion easier. Joe is insured by Imperial and his car is damaged. Sally is the other driver, and she is insured by another company. Not only is her car a total loss, she is in the hospital with neck and back injuries.

"So here's what we do," says a team member. "Joe calls up and says his car is damaged. We say, 'Oh, no, that's terrible. We'll have a replacement car at your house in an hour.' Is Joe happy? Thrilled. And we're saving money, because we're going to deliver Joe a mid-sized car, not the Lincoln he might have rented, and we're going to pay only $10 a day for it, not the $30 a day it would have cost him."

Nor does the team forget about Sally. Imperial isn't her insurer, but at this point who knows who's going to have to pay? What does the company want to be to Sally at this point? Warm, the group decides—a friend. Sally needs to see a kind and sympathetic person from Imperial in her hospital room. The explicit message will be, we're here to help. The implicit message? Don't sue. Also, maybe if we provide Sally such good service, she will switch to us. So claims processing becomes a sales opportunity.

One thing that customers like, someone says, is not having to deal with lots of different people on a claim. "What if we could make it so they had to deal with only one person?" "Okay, what if we did?" responds the captain. The team discusses creating something they call a case manager. Sally's in the hospital, and she's concerned about her car. The case manager will take care of it for her.

Sally has a bunch of different doctors, but none of them is going to solve her nonmedical problems. The case manager can. And by being on top of the situation, the team captain points out, the case manager can make sure that Sally gets good but not unnecessary medical care, which means that the company saves money again.

That's as far as the reengineering team got in its first redesign session. The team members haven't finished by any means. They still have lots of numbers to analyze and details to check, but they did get a good day's work done. They got over the first big hump, which is the challenge of coming up with big ideas. They didn't get mired in the old conventions. They were able to color outside the lines, to think outside of the box. And the team captain was good at provoking team members to speak up with ideas that might have seemed absurd on their face—the idea, for instance, of letting body shops settle small repair claims for clients without company investigation and appraisals. "How interesting," the captain said, inviting other team members to carry the idea even further.

In that instance, the team members were employing a technique that we often find useful. They were carrying a principle of reengineering—one that says work is best organized around outcomes, not tasks—to its logical extreme just to see where it leads. As a result they got a good idea, the one involving body shops.

Let's examine how the team might have applied another reengineering principle to guide them in their effort. The one we show here is by no means the only principle we might use; indeed, the ongoing discovery and articulation of the principles underlying reengineered processes is one of our major continuing efforts. Nonetheless, the following illustrates how applying new design principles can spark powerful ideas.

Principle: As few people as possible should be involved in the performance of a process.

Not all redesigned work processes end up in the hands of a single worker, but that isn't a bad goal for which to strive. Imagine that only one person is available to handle an insurance claim. What tasks would have to be eliminated or combined to make that possible? What work would have to be shifted outside—to the body shop, for instance? Had the reengineering team at Imperial Insurance applied this one-worker assumption, it could have triggered the idea of a case manager. More generally, imagine that only a single person is available to perform all the tasks involved in building a product. How would he or she be likely to do it? What help would that single worker need? How could technology lend a hand? These are the kinds of questions that will generate big ideas.

Asking themselves questions based on this and other principles of reengineering and seeing where the answers lead them is one technique that reengineering team members can use to get the redesign process moving. The objective of raising such questions is not to produce final answers but to stimulate the group's creative juices.

Another technique that we often find useful in stimulating the reengineering team members' thinking is that of identifying and annihilating assumptions.

Assumptions are deeply held beliefs that underlie and are built into almost every existing business process. If, for instance, field salespeople are not allowed to set the terms of the deal, it is a consequence of the assumption that salespeople put their own financial interests ahead of the company's in order to get a commission. The practice of paying suppliers only after receiving their invoices is based on an assumption that it would be impossible to correlate received goods directly with purchase orders. If a company maintains regional distribution centers, it may be because it assumes that regional centers provide better service than a centralized distribution operation.

A reengineering team can try turning these assumptions on their heads or throwing them out entirely and see where that leaves the process they are redesigning.

The Imperial Insurance team implicitly questioned the assumption that all body shops overcharge to see what steps or tasks in the process that might allow them to eliminate. They also determined what needed to be done to make the assumption invalid (in this case, it was the periodic monitoring of body shop performance).

The Imperial team also questioned the assumption that fault had to be determined before anyone could get paid. The result was a streamlined and faster process.

One of the T-shirt slogans of the 1960s read "Question authority." Process owners might buy their reengineering team members the new version: "Question assumptions."

A third technique that reengineering teams can use to stimulate their own creativity is to harness the disruptive power of information technology.

As we stressed in Chapter 5, conventional business process structures reflect the limitations of the precomputer era technologies on which the designs of these processes were based. The limitations of those technologies—the number of carbon copies a typist could produce or the amount of information one could send between headquarters and field offices through the mail or over the telephone—are deeply embedded in existing processes. When we try to improve these processes, we are still too often constrained by these same limitations.

Reengineering teams can break out of this bind by starting with the capabilities of modern information technology. See what technology allows you to do, and then determine if this helps you rethink the process.

For example, on-line computer databases allow Imperial to check easily on the claims-filing history of any particular customer and on the nature and cost of the repairs for which the company has paid various auto repair shops. With that never-before-available capability in mind, Imperial's reengineering team could reshape the damage-appraisal process, which was time-consuming, expensive, and damaging to the company's relationships with its claimant customers.

We have mentioned three kinds of techniques that reengineering teams can use to help them get the ideas flowing: boldly apply one or more principles of reengineering; search out and destroy assumptions; and go looking for opportunities for the creative application of technology. As redesign proceeds, teams can come back to these techniques to stimulate additional thought or get themselves over a hump.

Although Imperial Insurance is a fictitious company, the ideas we mentioned in the discussion are all plausible. Everything the Imperial reengineering team thought of is currently under consideration or implementation at a real insurance company.

Beyond the specific techniques noted above, the Imperial case teaches other important lessons about reengineering. In seminars, we often ask participants to play the roles of the Imperial reengineering team members. Afterward, we ask them to reflect on the experience that they have just had and tell us what else, besides the three techniques, they have learned about the experience of redesign. It's uncanny how often we get the same eight answers. Here's what the role players usually say they have discovered:

1. You don't need to be an expert to redesign a process.
2. Being an outsider helps.
3. You have to discard preconceived notions.
4. It's important to see things through the customer's eyes.
5. Redesign is best done in teams.
6. You don't need to know much about the current process.
7. It's not hard to have great ideas.
8. Redesign can be fun.

Redesign can be fun, but eventually comes the sobering moment when the reengineering team has to explain what it's been doing to the rest of the company—to the people who will have to adjust to and live with the team's redesigned processes. The team has to move from having ideas to making them happen. That part of the reengineering process can be less fun.

CHAPTER 9

EMBARKING ON REENGINEERING

We have held off until now discussing a crucial aspect of reengineering, one that actually has to begin at the very outset of the effort. The reason we have waited until this point, by which readers have acquired a grasp of the power and immensity of reengineering as a tool for reinventing companies, is that otherwise the significance of this deferred topic would have been easy to miss. What we are now discussing is the tremendous challenge of persuading the people within an organization to embrace—or at least not to fight—the prospect of major change.

Getting people to accept the idea that their work lives—their jobs—will undergo radical change is not a war won in a single battle. It is an educational and communications campaign that runs from reengineering's start to its finish. It is a selling job that begins with the realization that reengineering is required and doesn't wind down until well after the redesigned processes have been put into place.

In our experience, the companies that have the most success in selling change to their employees are those that have developed the clearest messages about the need for reengineering. Senior managers in these companies have done the best job of formulating, and articulating two key messages that they must communicate to the people who work in their organizations. The first of these is: Here is where we are as a company and this is why we can't stay here. The second is: This is what we as a company need to become.

The first message must make a compelling argument for change. It must convey a forceful message that reengineering is essential to the company's survival. This is a crucial requirement because employees who aren't convinced of the need for change will be disinclined to tolerate it and may even obstruct it. The process of developing this argument has the additional benefit of forcing management to look honestly at the company and its performance in the context of a broad competitive environment.

The second message, what the company needs to become, gives employees a palpable goal to shoot for. Articulating it forces management to think clearly about the purpose of their change program and about the extent of the change that needs to be effected through reengineering.

We have names for the documents that companies typically use to articulate and communicate these two essential messages. We call the first a "case for action" and the second a "vision statement." The names themselves are not important—various companies have given them different names—but the contents matter a great deal.

The case for action says *why* the company must reengineer. It has to be concise, comprehensible, and compelling. It can't just be management crying "Wolf!" It has to be a case for action—a dramatically persuasive argument, supported by evidence, that spells out the cost of doing anything short of reengineering. If a company stands to lose its competitive advantage in a particular line of business, the case for action should say so. If the company is seeing a steady erosion of its profit margins, the case for action should show that. If a company faces outright failure, the case for action should argue that, too—but only if it is true. The document must present a strong case, but it cannot exaggerate. The case for action must be so persuasive that no one in the organization will think that there is any alternative to reengineering. Most of the facts in the case for action probably won't be newly discovered, but by capturing them in a single document, the case for action makes people see that the organization is indeed broken.

The case for action should be brief—five to ten pages at most—and blunt. We admire the one that follows, which senior managers of a major pharmaceutical company prepared to convince their employees that the organization's research and development process had to be radically altered. This case for action contains all the elements we think are important, and it presents them economically.

CASE FOR ACTION: PHARMACEUTICAL COMPANY

We are disappointed by the length of time we require to develop and register new drugs in the United States and in major international markets.

Our leading competitors achieve significantly shorter development cycles because they've established larger-scale, highly flexible, globally integrated R&D organizations that operate with a uniform set of work practices and information systems.

The competitive trend goes against our family of smaller, independent R&D organizations, which are housed in several decentralized operating companies around the world.

We have strong competitive and economic incentives to move as quickly as possible toward a globally integrated model of operation: Each week we save in the development and registration process extends the commercial life of our patent protection and represents, at minimum, an additional $1 million in annual pretax profit—for each drug in our portfolio.

The previous case has five major elements that appear in most effective cases for action.

The *business context* summarizes and describes what is happening, what is changing, and what is newly important in the environment in which the company operates. Our leading competitors, this company's case for action says, are establishing much shorter development cycles.

The *business problem* is the source of the organization's concern. Our company, the document frankly admits, takes too long to develop and register new drugs.

The case for action also spells out *marketplace demands*—that is, how the contextual conditions have led to new performance requirements that the company can't meet. The competitive trend goes against our approach to research and development, this part says.

The *diagnostics* section of the case for action makes clear why the company is unable to meet the new performance requirements and why the usual fix-up, patch-up techniques of incremental improvement won't do. In this instance, the pharmaceutical company is losing its competitive edge to companies with globally integrated R&D organizations.

Finally, to eliminate any doubt about the need for reengineering, the case for action ends with a section that warns of the consequences of not reengineering, the *costs of inaction*. We stand to lose $1 million in annual profits per drug for every week's delay in development and registration, this part says.

A company doesn't have to teeter on the verge of bankruptcy to make a compelling case for reengineering. A case for action can be made even for a company that is doing well. Such an organization can argue that if it doesn't reengineer it *will* be in trouble, that it isn't as good as the market *will* demand that it be, or that it isn't as good as it has decided it *wants* to be. These are harder cases to make, which only means that the case for action has to be all the more compellingly argued.

Here's a case for action used by a consumer products company that is still profitable. The statement paints a dismal picture of the company's future if it doesn't reengineer. This case for action is longer than the pharmaceutical company's, but it is equally effective. It begins with an overview of the company's industry.

CASE FOR ACTION: CONSUMER PRODUCTS COMPANY

Markets are changing so quickly in our retail channels that, in order to generate profitable growth for our distributors, we must be able to respond quickly with exactly the right programs.

Each of our channels has unique needs for innovative products, services, promotion, merchandising systems, and training to enable them to compete and succeed in their markets. We must develop the flexible processes within our company that thrive on these channel-specific opportunities.

Consumer needs and desires are constantly changing, based on new retail formats, media stimulation, new products/substitute products, changing lifestyles, and market segmentation. We cannot develop a product concept or retail solution that appeals to everyone; products that are highly successful with one market segment will be rejected by another.

Next, it logically examines in competitive terms the factors that argue for change.

Today, the time that elapses between our assessing a marketplace need and our delivery of a new program at retail is at least two years and can stretch out as long as three. Furthermore, the process is largely sequential. Each of the steps—interpreting retail and research data; developing plans; obtaining commitments; and getting agreement on product, merchandising, promotion, advertising, systems, training, and field-launch plans—crosses many division lines and requires endless meetings and approvals.

In a dynamic market, a three-year planning cycle is unacceptable. Even if a product or program seems innovative in the early planning stages, it no longer is when it reaches the consumer twenty-four or thirty-six months later. Feedback on retail performance comes too late to affect replacement products and leaves poor performers in the market too long.

Frequently, the scope of our planning and decision-making process is too narrow and does not encompass multiple channels or specific retailers. These are often left out or added late in the process, when our options are limited.

Many times, when programs arrive at retail, the order is late, products and merchandising are missing, and the retailer or field personnel lack enough training to effectively install or sell it.

The consumer product company's case winds up by emphatically stating the consequences of not reengineering:

The current process is incapable of meeting our growing need for speed and precision. It produces, instead, a stressed and overworked staff, last-minute scrambles, increasing exception processing, and creaky systems. Our current process costs the company millions of dollars in overtime and excess expenses, missed deliveries, and less-than-acceptable retailer performance and confidence.

We often place our focus on maximizing our own cost-effectiveness rather than on marketplace needs and performance. We have applied technology to improving what we do with little result. We have measured success by our own internal performance, rather than by our retailers' yardsticks.

Just working harder and more efficiently within our existing process won't get us to our goal of dramatically improving retail performance.

We're still very profitable today, but if we don't take comprehensive remedial actions soon, our continued success is at risk. Without major change, we will eventually fail.

This company's case for action, incidentally, led to a comprehensive and effective reengineering effort.

We have said there are two key components of the larger message that senior management has to communicate to the organization to get reengineering underway. The first is the "let's change" part—the case for action; the second is "to what"—the vision.

The case for action paints with a broad brush the nature of the company's business problem. "We have to get change going," it says. The vision says, "Here is what we want to be." It depicts the destination of the reengineering effort.

The vision statement, by that or any other name, is the way a company's management communicates a sense of the kind of organization the company needs to become. It describes how the company is going to operate and outlines the kind of results it must achieve. It is both a qualitative and a quantitative statement, which a company can use again and again before and during reengineering, as a reminder of reengineering's objectives, as a yardstick for measuring progress, and as a prod to keep the reengineering action going.

Creating the vision of a reengineered organization requires some artistry, because a vision is an image without great detail. When a company is taking its first steps toward reengineering, no one really knows exactly where it is heading; no one really knows exactly what it will become; no one really even knows which aspects of the current company will change, let alone precisely how. The vision is what a company believes it *wants* to achieve when it is done, and a well-drawn vision will sustain a company's resolve through the stress of the reengineering process.

The vision can act as a flag around which to rally the troops when morale starts to sag. "Remember how great it will be when we get there," the flag says to them. The vision also provides a continuing focus. It reminds people constantly of what it is the company is trying to change. Otherwise, people easily become sidetracked and diverted. In any company at any time, countless procedures and organizational details exist that *could* be changed. The vision reminds the organization which processes will actually need to be worked.

Finally, the vision provides a yardstick for measuring the progress of reengineering. Does the company look like its vision yet? If it is getting closer, reengineering is making progress. If not, then no matter how much effort has gone into reengineering, it hasn't created the progress on which the company is counting. Holding up the vision, the leader can say, "This is what we have agreed we want to be. Look around. Are we there yet? Are we close?" The vision is a useful prod. And, if it's really powerful, it creates a pull.

By working with companies that are reengineering their processes, we have expressed vision statements in some corny but effective ways. For instance, with desktop publishing it is easy to dummy up a *Wall Street Journal* article about the company written, say, five years hence. The story we write might say that the company has achieved record profits and jumped to the top of its industry by dramatically shortening its product development cycle. Then the story might spin out how it feels to work for the company and what customers and employees think about the changes it has made. This kind of device captures employees' imaginations. "Yes," they say, "we would like that." Well, that is the dream, the leader can say, and here is what we have to do to make it real.

Used together, the case for action and the vision work like a wedge and a magnet. To get people to move from where they are to where they are supposed to be requires two actions. First, they have to get unstuck from where they are. The tool that unsticks people is a wedge—the case for action. Next, the unstuck people have to be attracted to another point of view. That is the job of a magnet—the vision.

Vision statements need not be long, but they have to be powerful. Too many corporate visions tend to the vacuous and simplistic and provide no clue as to what the company must do to achieve them. "We want to be number one in our industry" or "We want to be the premier manufacturer of widgets" or "We will be the preferred supplier for our customers" are nice wishes, but they are not useful visions. Statements such as these often stem from the annual walk in the woods—those occasions when company executives go on retreat, claim to reexamine their purpose, and draw up what they term a vision statement. Although they are well intended, such statements are devoid of any real meaning. They don't suggest concretely how the company wants to operate, they have no real utility, and they wear off very quickly.

A powerful vision contains three elements that a product of a walk in the woods usually lacks. First, it focuses on operations; second, it includes measurable objectives and metrics; and third, if it is really powerful, it changes the basis for competition in the industry.

One of the best and simplest examples of a vision we know was expressed by Federal Express in its infancy: "We will deliver the package by 10:30 the next morning." That statement is about operations (we will get the package delivered); it has measurable objectives (we will deliver it by 10:30 A.M.); and it changed the basis of competition in the industry (from long, unpredictable delivery times to guaranteed overnight delivery). Federal Express's vision statement told people in the company that they had to design their work to accomplish that objective.

Vision statements can be much longer, as the samples below illustrate, without being soft. These sample vision statements have sharp edges, they contain no platitudes, and they include the three key elements we have just discussed. Here, to start, is the pharmaceutical company's vision of its drug development process in its reengineered incarnation.

VISION: PHARMACEUTICAL COMPANY
We are a worldwide leader in drug development.
• We have shortened drug development and registration by an average of six months.
• We are an acknowledged leader in the quality of registration submissions.

- We have maximized the profit potential of our development portfolio.

We have created, across our operating companies, a worldwide R&D organization with management structures and systems that let us mobilize our collective development resources responsively and flexibly.

- We have established uniform and more disciplined drug development planning, decision making, and operational processes across all sites.
- We employ innovative technology-based tools to support our work and management practices at all levels and between all R&D sites.
- We have developed and implemented a common information technology architecture worldwide.

The consumer products firm whose case for action we looked at earlier has also articulated its end-state vision.

VISION: CONSUMER PRODUCTS FIRM

Operating close to the marketplace injects a new life into the entire product development process. We develop plans, make decisions, produce products, and launch programs with a sense of immediacy. Our employees are rewarded by seeing products in stores that they worked on weeks or months but not years ago.

Our market focus is sharpened because our fully integrated programs are never more than a year away from market. The needs of our marketplace drive us, and we evaluate our success by our performance at retail—retail sales, retail profitability, retail service, and retail execution.

Cross-divisional teams working simultaneously streamline the development planning process. Priorities are consistent across all divisions as we focus our efforts on programs that move the needle. We set clear objectives, and market research provides immediate feedback on how well we performed against these objectives.

The freshness of our product offering and the cohesive merchandising presentation and execution give all our retailers a competitive edge. Our field organization and accounts are fully trained in the process of implementation and in the strategies supporting our programs so that they can sell to their customers knowledgeably and enthusiastically.

Our retailers can see that our programs are forward-looking, aggressive, and right for them. They notice the impact on their sales and profits immediately. Our products arrive complete, on time, and packed for efficient checkin and setup. Those responsible for merchandising these products have all the necessary tools and training. The partnership between us and our retailers is so strong that we work toward the same objectives and the same measures of success.

We have said that preparing and disseminating the case for action and the vision is the first step in reengineering. It is the leader's personal responsibility to articulate and communicate these key messages. It is only an individual with the leader's seniority and clout who can fashion and communicate these critical arguments.

The senior management team—the leader's peers or reports—represent the first audience for these messages. These messages are not easy for them to hear, since they say that the organization these people head is in need of major change. Only a very senior executive has the credibility and the clout to make such an assertion. An outside agent—a consultant—can be of help in this step, since an agent has no biases or vested interests and can be seen as an objective third party. Telling senior managers that their company is broken is difficult, since they have, in fact, played a substantial role in creating the current company, so diplomacy as well as credibility are important in communicating the case for action and the vision to them.

After senior management hears these messages, the rest of the organization must get the word, too. The case for action and the vision are the opening salvos in an ongoing communication barrage to enlist the entire organization in the reengineering crusade.

In the following three chapters, we will look at very different companies and see how they have been able to launch and sustain successful reengineering efforts.

CHAPTER 10

ONE COMPANY'S EXPERIENCE: DUKE POWER

On the surface, Duke Power Company had little reason to undertake reengineering in 1995. Its quality of customer service seemed adequately high, and its energy costs were among the lowest in the nation. Other electric utilities would have been content with Duke Power's level of performance.

But as successful companies know, a hallmark of leadership is the willingness to take risks in order to achieve even more. Duke Power is such a company. Long recognized as an industry leader, it has received numerous awards for efficiency, customer service, and environmental stewardship.

Indeed, in 1999, Duke Energy (the company created by the 1997 merger of Duke Power and midstream natural gas company Pan Energy) was named by *Fortune* as the country's most admired gas and electric company. Little wonder, then, that the utility, based in Charlotte, North Carolina, took action when power deregulation first seemed possible. Richard B. Priory, then president of Duke Power and now chairman, president, and CEO of Duke Energy, recognized that the utility needed to cut costs and further improve its customer service if it wanted to remain competitive when deregulation arrived.

Priory started the wheels turning, but it was Jimmy R. Hicks, senior vice president of retail services, who recognized that a new kind of organization offered the best chance of achieving Priory's goals. And it was Hicks who, with the help of E. O. Ferrell III, senior vice president of electric distribution, did the hands-on work necessary to make reengineered customer operations a reality at Duke Power.

In the pages that follows, Hicks and Ferrell explain what the old organization was like. They also share their day-to-day experiences in the reengineering of Duke Power.

Hicks: In late 1994, I left our company's information technology department to take over its customer operations organization—what we call retail services. Customer operations takes in all the employees within the towns and cities that we serve who are needed to transfer the energy from the high-voltage system, often called the grid, to the customer.

In other words, customer operations is the heart, soul, and muscle in delivering energy to Duke Power's customers. These are the people who run, bury, and maintain the lines up and down your street. They read your meter, send your bill, collect your money, and figure out what rate you're going to pay for all this service. They are the conduits, if you will, between the raw electricity and the customer at home.

Certain that deregulation was on the way, our president and my boss, Rick Priory, determined that we needed to cut our cost of delivery, while simultaneously improving the quality of service, if we wanted to be ready for the competition. Our quality of service was already pretty high, but Rick set a goal of service in the upper quartile among electric utilities in our area. Once we started to look, we found plenty of opportunities for improvement.

Ferrell: For instance, under the old system, a customer would call in and request a service visit that would print out at an operating center. We serve 2 million customers spread over 20,000 square miles in North and South Carolina, so those operating centers were all over the place.

An administrative representative took the request from the printer and placed it in a box based on the day the job was to be performed. Then the request was transferred into a front-line worker's box on the day it was supposed to be done.

All those handoffs were just to start a job. And even worse, no one made any attempt to determine whether a particular job would take one hour or two hours or whatever. So, some workers were sent out with only five or six hours of work, while others had more than they could possibly complete in one day.

Hicks: The signposts were clear: To meet the challenge of lowering costs while improving service, we could no longer manage our work functions in this way.

Before coming to customer operations from information technology, I had already started thinking and reading more about processes and how one reengineers around them. It seemed to me that approaching work from the perspective of processes would solve the problems we were facing.

At about the same time, we realized we needed to replace our antiquated customer information system, which dated back to 1971. Eager for ideas, we hired consultants to help us select an appropriate new system.

In so doing, we reviewed our work processes with the consultants. So we were already beginning to think in process terms and understand how ours operated, but we had not considered them fundamental to customer operations.

Ferrell: We simply had not focused on process. There was no consistent way of looking at process at Duke Power. We had thirteen geographical areas and did everything thirteen different ways, each with a little twist that fitted the politics of a particular area, the capabilities of particular employees, and the size of the organization in that area.

Any time you wanted to change something, you had to change it, literally, thirteen times, and everyone had at least as many reasons why that change would not work in such-and-such an area. As a result, nothing much was ever improved.

Pervading the inefficiencies was low morale. We had a series of layoffs over the five or six years before Jim began talking about restructuring, so just the mention of the word "reengineering" scared some people—not because they heard or read negative publicity, but because they assumed more layoffs were on the way.

"Do you folks know what you might do to this company?" colleagues asked us. "Our customers won't believe you can deliver services after this shake-up."

Stories floated around about companies that started to reengineer then quit. Some business thinkers I knew of believed reengineering was too tough to live through. Misinformation on the subject was rampant. In retrospect, if we were to start all over, we would start to educate everyone about reengineering sooner.

Hicks: To start the ball rolling—or maybe "kick off" is a better way to put it—we needed a game plan to sell this thing called reengineering, and a game needs players, team players. In hindsight, it really was like a football game, where so much depends on people working together to achieve a common goal.

Think of it this way. In football, you have an offensive coordinator who looks after the whole offense, and you have a similar defensive coordinator. In addition, you have coaches who teach players how to work, and you have the players, themselves, who execute individual plans in the service of an overall strategy.

That is how a process organization works, too. There are players who execute maintenance work, those who execute new customer work, those who deal with problems as they arise, and so on. They must all interface with one another. The manager's job is to teach them the processes. Once people viewed our game plan in terms of football, they began to understand it.

We started by defining and analyzing primary customer service operations in terms of five major processes, each with a process owner who was responsible for the design of the work and the resources it required. The processes were these.

1. *Developing market strategies.* This means figuring out what customers want, creating that product, pricing it, and setting a target market share.

2. *Acquiring and maintaining the customer.* This entails all the interaction with the customer, from selling the product to keeping the customer happy by answering service questions, and so forth.

3. *Delivering products and services.* Once a product is invented and sold to a customer, the company has to provide what it has promised. It must be built with quality and delivered on time.

4. *Calculating and collecting.* After an order is completed, you must bill the customer and, of course, get paid.

5. *Managing the delivery system.* It is critical that an electrical infrastructure work correctly, so that customers have power 24 hours a day, 7 days a week, 365 days a year. So we created a process that ensures smooth, continuous service.

Eventually, we added a sixth process to these five: *supporting the business*, which includes all the support it takes to keep information technology, finance, and human resources operating without a hitch.

Once we defined and analyzed these six processes, everyone could understand the concept of process-managed work. In addition, we could see how to go about actually reengineering the activities that make up the processes.

Ferrell: Reengineering means fundamentally changing the way you provide service—and value—to the customer. After identifying and mapping the basic processes, you try to take advantage of information technology to minimize the number of handoffs, eliminate steps, and widen your current span of control.

In other words, you put information in the hands of front-line performers, who can serve the customer with a minimal amount of guidance or supervision. The result is that employees can respond to customers on the spot. In addition, the company saves money because fewer people are involved in the process.

Jim Hicks was the one with the vision and the commitment to push process reengineering from the top down. But as part of his initial leadership team and as the process owner responsible for delivering products and services, I had to analyze and develop the activities that unfold from the moment a customer calls to say, "I want service to my new house" until the power usage is determined by the meter reader. My span of responsibility covered all the new business expansion activity and all of the operation and maintenance activities for 2 million customers.

We discovered numerous problems when we mapped these processes, most of which revolved around the fragmented way we had been working. The fragmentation was embedded in the organization's culture, which we needed to change.

Hicks: Mapping the processes clearly pointed up our inefficient operating structure. As a result, we decided to separate
the strategic work from the tactical work. No longer were the
same people trying to operate the day-to-day business while
also trying to figure out how to solve tomorrow's problems.

We told the people in the field that their job was to execute
the processes as well as they could, while responsibility for
redesigning the process and managing the resources it required
was allocated to the process owner.

All of the processes were mapped out to highlight the inter-
connections between the output of one process, the input of
another, and the effect on the customer. Also, each process was
measured in a way that kept the customer at the center. For
example, a billing process was measured in terms of accuracy.

Very quickly, we learned that our existing measurement system was woefully inadequate. We developed a method that
linked our high-level goals—higher earnings and better service—to the people working in the field. That way they could
see the connection between their actions and, ultimately, the
overall costs, as well as the levels of customer satisfaction.

We know, of course, that one thing a company can do to
increase earnings is to increase revenues—and holding onto current customers makes top-line growth much easier. But in order
to do that, you must provide service that is accessible to measurement, whether the results rate that service as satisfactory or not.

Our problem was that when customers told us they wanted
malfunctioning streetlights repaired within three days, we
realized that in fact, we had no idea how long it usually took to
repair lights. But we decided that didn't matter. Since three
days was important to our customers, we set a standard that 95
percent of lights would be repaired within three days. We estimated that 5 percent of malfunctioning streetlights are usually
caused by underground problems for which you have to bring
in heavy equipment to dig big holes. This is very hard to do in

three days. But we thought that the other 95 percent could be dealt with in three days.

Now, when a technician goes out to repair a light, he or she knows that if it is accomplished within three days, customer satisfaction will be high—maybe 9 on a scale of 1 to 10. We monitored customer satisfaction, and the technician knows that happy customers create revenues.

Ferrell: That's right. We track customer satisfaction, and the payback has been enormous. Here's just one example of how things have improved.

Let's say that a customer wants the power turned off at 1234 Chambers Street on Monday and wants it turned on at 456 Westfield Road, the same day. An order is created for each request.

When we began measuring, we discovered that we only completed orders within the promised period around 74 percent of the time.

As part of process reengineering, we instituted the "scorecard" concept, which sets specific goals for each process. One of them was that a minimum of 96 percent of orders had to be completed by the day they were promised. Within a recent twelve-month period, our crews completed 98 percent of their meter orders on or before the due date—not a bad record, we think.

Hicks: You can see how this system of measurement is a great incentive for getting work done quickly and efficiently, since both the process owner and his or her colleagues on the team know that customer satisfaction increases revenues. And the teams can see how measurements affect them individually when they get their monthly scorecards.

We have created a measurement system in which everyone can readily see the goal and act on this knowledge. An enormous part of a good reengineering effort focuses on making sure information is accessible and communicated. And through this measurement system, we relegate most of the responsibility for the actual delivery of service to the frontline worker. This didn't happen overnight, of course. It took months.

Once reengineering helped us understand our processes, we were able to measure them. Then we quantified those measurements in customer terms and gave this crucial feedback to the employees, who could see how they were meeting measurement standards and what the rewards were for doing so.

We also developed pay incentives—that is, achieve a certain level above the standard and you will be rewarded for it.

Ferrell: Nowhere are the speed and efficiency achieved by process reengineering at Duke Power more visible than in our scheduling activities. What a breakthrough it was when we came up with a system for determining how long a job should take.

We have various kinds of work, ranging from the heavy construction involved in setting up poles, pulling wire, hanging transformers, and the like to routine work, such as dealing with a customer's broken backyard light or a meter base that was pulled away from the house.

In response, we put together a guide that said, "This job ought to take fifteen minutes. This job ought to take thirty minutes," then, we began to build templates. Every morning we had the administrative team organize the work into packages that the workers would pick up when they came in. Quickly, we discovered that we were frequently sending people out for the day with less than a day's work.

We also began color-coding to designate levels of priority: yellow for work committed to the customer today, blue for work due within three days, and green for work that can be done any time. Previously, performers got their work orders, did whatever they could in one day, then, returned the remaining orders to their cubbyholes. Any leftover work could wait until tomorrow—or next week.

Now our schedulers, whom we call assemblers, put together packages of a full day's work that are distributed to employees with the expectation that it will all be finished on the appointed day.

We were shocked when we discovered our hidden capabilities. We could increase productivity without making folks work a lot harder. We just had to provide them with the opportunity to do a full day's work. With metrics to guide us, we were able to organize and synthesize a very basic set of steps so that we could do tasks the same way everywhere.

We also standardized trucks. Before, every line truck was outfitted differently, which worked fine as long as the same two people were always on the same truck. But if another crew came in and used this truck, they didn't know where things were.

Some line trucks had enough material on them to work for a week—they were like rolling storerooms—and others had very little. Now the trucks are virtually interchangeable.

Even the way we organize vacations has changed. Now, you don't just ask your supervisor for days off. Instead, processes exist for requesting vacation time, calling in sick, getting time off for doctors' appointments, and so on. The central office handles it. Schedulers can know in advance what the size of the workforce will be on any given day.

By removing the immediate supervisors from the scheduling process, we have standardized what was once a disorganized, unmethodical way of dealing with employees' absences. Before standardization, for example, one supervisor might send two performers out on a job that another supervisor knew could be done with one.

Hicks: The changes at Duke Power have certainly been worth the effort, but it wasn't easy going from a traditional, hierarchically managed organization to one where team playing is key.

We went from a top-down, chain-of-command view of the world to one that is matrix-managed—that is, process owners and geographical managers are jointly accountable for the work. Processes stretch horizontally across the work, while decision making is compressed vertically to become part of the work itself. No longer is it severed and directed upward to an overriding manager.

It was a huge cultural change for everyone. For example, our linemen were used to receiving work on a daily basis from their supervisors: "Here, Joe, you go do this."

In contrast, in process-managed work, the centralized scheduling system manages more effectively the amount of work that is to be completed on any given day. An assembler looks at the system and parcels out the work assignments to the frontline workers.

The supervisor's role has been transformed. Now, he or she is more of a facilitator who makes sure the worker has everything necessary to accomplish the assigned tasks.

The workers had to adjust to receiving their work from someone in a scheduling organization instead of from their supervisors—and they complained about it, by the way. "This guy in scheduling doesn't know what's going on out here. I'm used to dealing with my supervisor."

We have worked hard to overcome culture barriers like these, but we had to spend a great deal of time educating employees about process-managed work: why it works the way it does, what we expect from it, what our problems were and how reengineering would solve them, and why the old way of working would not solve those problems. We also had to do extra training about *how* you perform your new work process.

We brought in people from Hammer & Company, and they introduced us to a board game similar to Monopoly—another gaming metaphor and a great training tool. The game revolved around owning and operating an imaginary power company and making decisions with a roll of the dice.

Linemen who had never had to worry about the consequences of decision making spent a day working through the game and rolling the dice. You should have seen their faces when, all of a sudden, they realized that making a decision *not* to standardize something comes at a cost.

Though time-consuming and expensive, the training was worth it to help frontline workers understand the business implications of making decisions. We could not have succeeded without it.

You just can't go down this road that leads to transformation without making that level of investment. You have to convince people that what you want them to do is the right thing to do.

Ferrell: But once you've got the new organization in place, you've got a great platform for moving forward. The perspective that "we do the same job in the same way, everywhere," is of enormous value. You no longer have to deal with all the negative "that won't work here" comments. You no longer waste energy debating whether or not to do something.

We have been able to identify the opportunities and take advantage of them. For instance, in some areas we are holding the line on O&M cost per customer added, which means we are absorbing 2.5 percent customer growth along with inflation. Elsewhere, we have actually driven down the cost per customer added while absorbing inflation.

Our low costs have already put us in the top quartile among competitor utilities. We are shooting to move into the top decile, and I'm confident we can get there.

Hicks: For anyone who is considering or just starting a reengineering effort, it is important to realize that when you change your processes, not everything happens on day 1.

Work efficiency may go south for a while, as people learn new jobs and new processes. For example, the first scheduling system we had in place just didn't work right. The work wasn't getting done on time. As a consequence, valued relationships we had nurtured with home builders suffered.

We need to work very closely with builders during the construction of new homes, but while we were designing and refining our work processes, we damaged the trust and intimacy we had built up over the years.

Our field supervisors were gone, and this led to miscommunication. People moved into houses that had not had the electricity hooked up yet, and buildings remained unfinished. Our old friends, the builders, were saying, "You're not delivering the service. We don't know who to talk to anymore!" It was a terrible situation.

Still, true reengineering never quits. We had to review our processes for delivering services to those builders and then explain to them what was going on. We also came up with some new options, like faxing in applications, which was easier for them. Things are improving, but we are still working to mend our relationships with contractors.

It is good to remember that the best-laid plans don't always work in the real world the way they do on paper. And sometimes relationships become very strained before issues can be worked through. So you have to be strong-willed—and thick-skinned—to shepherd through changes like the ones we undertook. There is no question that change can be painful.

At certain times, the repercussions were such that we had to question whether we were moving too far, too fast. E. O. and I would look at each other and say, "Are we doing the right thing?" But we both genuinely believed we were, so we bolstered each other's confidence to continue and complete this project.

I believe you can implement changes like these in one of two ways. You can say, "Okay, we have designed this process-based work and the organization we need to execute it. We can take a year or two to implement it fully, moving people around as opportunities arise, build gradual acceptance, and make a transition that is relatively smooth."

Or you can jump in with both feet and say, "Let's reengineer today! Let's staff the organization the way we know it should be and do it within the next thirty days. Then that new organization will manage this transition."

I chose the more radical method, even though we were far from sure about how to do many of the things that we knew we were going to do. It meant making organizational change right away, but I wanted to impart a sense of urgency about getting things done. And I wanted to burn bridges behind us. If you make a more gradual transition, people will try to slide back into doing things the way they did them before.

With the institution of a process-based organization, we were able to eliminate our middle layer of management. Some of these individuals found jobs in other parts of the corporation. We worked out a very nice benefits package for the others. All told, we eliminated 130 to 140 positions out of 4,500, none of which were frontline jobs.

Moving so fast was like ripping off the bandages after surgery: It stings, but the quicker you do it, the quicker it is over.

Then we were able to focus on our future as a process-based organization. We could not go back to the old way, because those employees and their positions were gone. We had to make the new processes work, and this created a sense of commitment.

The most difficult thing was getting the frontline performers to believe that the system would work. It took much longer than I expected. A case in point is what happened with our decision to standardize company trucks, which E.O. talked about earlier.

As he explained, our linemen had set these vehicles up to suit their own personal tastes. But making them interchangeable allowed us to cut our fleet size without risking our efficiency during emergencies or when the trucks were being serviced.

Our linemen, however, were upset. They were very attached to their particular vehicles and fought hard against the idea. "It won't work! When I go out there, I won't have the material I need," they said. Or we heard, "That was *my* truck. I operated it. I kept it clean. What you've given me doesn't feel like mine anymore!"

The outcry was so strong that I began to question the decision to standardize, but eventually we used the feedback to modify the way the trucks were set up. That we listened and acted on the workers' complaints helped resolve the angry feelings.

The fact is, there will always be resistance to change. But if you are determined to make the changes work, it is no longer an insurmountable issue.

Ferrell: I agree that persistence is crucial. To be successful, you have to be stubborn and consistent.

Still, in retrospect, we probably didn't always communicate as well as we should have. We did a lot of good things, but I think we could have done a better job of articulating a clear vision of what we wanted to achieve and then communicating it to all employees. Perhaps, we could have better explained why change was necessary, what it would mean; we could have painted a picture of what the organization would look like after we got through the rough seas.

Also, it is important to manage the implementation so that you have some early successes, and we did not do that as well as we might have. We are engineers. We wanted to bite off the whole thing and make it work. We should have realized that the sooner you can encourage the troops with visible results, the better off you are.

We did roll out process-managed work separately in four regions, each serving about a half million customers, and that helped. The first region became our lab. They were adamant that they could see the benefits of reengineering and that it was going to work. So whenever I had problems elsewhere, I was able to point to the improvements we were seeing in the first region.

Hicks: Part of the dissonance we experienced with the linemen, and with other areas too, is what I like to call "constructive tension."

When you set up an organization that is process-managed, and you have process owners who control the design and the resources required, there is bound to be tension with the people in the field who have to execute the changes. They see the processes from a different perspective.

One person will say, "If you execute this right, you can do it with ten people." And the guy out in the field might say, "There is no way I can do this with ten people. It'll take sixteen." Time to take a deep breath! Everyone has to sit down and figure out the final number.

Companies can profit from constructive tension. Without it, you're going to have a process that is driven too much either by the process owner's viewpoint or by that of the frontline performers. The process owner is trying to accomplish the job while driving down costs, and performers fear being overworked and underpaid. Only with constructive tension can everyone determine where the balance is.

As we saw at Duke Power, it isn't easy to change the culture of a corporation. Unless it is pushed from the top, it won't get done. My role was to push. Most importantly, my job was to convince the new layer of process owners that we were engaged in the right effort. I helped with their design work, and together we yoked a team capable of speeding the plow.

During the transitional period, I spent two days a week—it probably *should* have been four—out in the field, providing leadership, and working on finding a proper balance between process owners and frontline workers. I was as visible as I felt I could be at the time, but if I had it to do over again, I would increase my presence.

The leader needs to encourage each and every employee, telling him or her what is being done right, even though people feel that the world is falling down around them. Let them know that you're willing to learn, and that you will make progress together.

Eventually, everything fell into place. The reengineering effort determined the work processes, which we mapped out on paper. Every employee came to understand them.

Looking back on our experiences, I think what was most critical to our success was selecting the process owners early on. Choosing the right people is so important. You need a blend of personalities, people who are unafraid to confront, or even instigate, constructive creative tension.

Another key element is having a knowledgeable, independent facilitator who can show how process management works elsewhere. A dispassionate facilitator will help you raise critical issues and work through resistance.

Ferrell: Today, the mood around Duke Power is better than it has been in years. All the customer surveys are high and getting higher. For two consecutive years, *Fortune* magazine rated us "best in customer satisfaction" at an electrical utility.

We are not ready to rest on our laurels. We have recently undertaken a reengineering effort within the company's engineering group.

We have come a long way, but we continue to search for new ways to improve a process and take advantage of advancements in technology.

Right now we are installing mobile data terminals inside our trucks, which means we will reduce the areas in which we have dispatchers from twenty to four. And we will eliminate the manual retyping of orders into the computer, because when an order is completed on the truck terminal, it will automatically go back to the mainframe. That is reengineering, too.

Most importantly, perhaps, our confidence and our ability to tackle cultural change are much greater than they were just a few years ago.

This confidence permeates our leadership. It is evident in the fearless way we say, "We have done it before, and we can do it again—and again and again."

Many of the themes in the Duke Power experience should be familiar by now, but the story also raises some novel issues. The first relates to the very notion of process, which underlies the entire edifice of reengineering.

Most companies see process as an antidote to the fragmentation induced by deteriorating functional organizations, and they're right. But it has another dimension, which looms large in the Duke Power story: consistency and discipline.

Prior to reengineering, Duke Power's processes were performed differently, and largely on an ad hoc basis, in its thirteen geographical areas. There were few formal, and no standard, process designs. The inevitable result was inefficient and inconsistent performance.

Enter reengineering.

At Duke Power, reengineering not only improved process designs, it introduced the notion of processes with designs. Reengineering formalized and standardized Duke Power's processes, thereby creating order out of chaos. Work is now done deliberately and predictably, not extemporaneously.

At this company, as everywhere else, the most difficult and challenging parts of the reengineering effort centered on human issues, not on technical ones. Jim Hicks and E. O. Ferrell tell us that success requires leaders to be persistent, stubborn, and consistent—leaders who will not back down in the face of resistance or difficulty. Clear communication throughout the organization is a prerequisite for progress in a reengineering effort. Also, the project should be planned to achieve some early success, which will build momentum and create enthusiasm. Hicks and Ferrell promote the strategy of burning one's bridges and making drastic changes. That way it is evident to everyone that there is no turning back and the only path is forward.

The Duke Power story offers a good reminder of the importance of education in reengineering. Reengineered processes are streamlined and have little non-value-adding overhead, so few managers are going to track what people are doing. (It is not uncommon, as happened at Duke Power, for traditional management roles to be decreased, if not eliminated.) People who work in these processes must be empowered and autonomous and have the business knowledge to make their own decisions, rather than running to the boss. Duke Power invested substantially in an educational program precisely for this, and it has proven well worth the effort. Duke Power's leaders emphasize that education is the antidote to the confusion and misinformation that may surround the term "reengineering."

The most distinctive aspect of Duke Power's experience is that it is only partly about reengineering. It is equally about the aftermath of reengineering, the new kind of organization that arises in the wake of a serious and sustained reengineering program. As a reengineering leader at Texas Instruments once noted, "You can't overlay high-performance processes on a functional organization."

Reengineered processes are based on cross-functional teams of empowered workers, who will always be unnatural phenomena in a traditional, functional, hierarchical organization. In the long run, reengineered processes can only thrive in a *process-centered organi-*

zation: one in which process owners are not transient project managers, but key executives charged with assuring the long-term health of the processes; where measurement systems focus not on functional performance, but on total process performance; where people's compensation is linked to how well their processes perform; and where all people understand the company's processes, and how their individualized work contributes to realizing the company's goals. (The process-centered organization is discussed in detail in Michael Hammer's 1996 book *Beyond Reengineering*.) Most companies, perhaps wisely, decide to evolve to such process-centered organizations, first reengineering their processes, integrating the benefits of their improved performance, and then aligning the organization around them.

Duke Power opted for a more dramatic approach. The company first reorganized around its processes and then redesigned and reimplemented them. This is not necessarily the right approach for everyone, but it has paid off handsomely for Duke Power. Not only has the performance of individual processes excelled, but Duke Power as a whole leads the pack in the complex, deregulating world of electric power. The company is achieving high customer satisfaction at low cost, a neat trick in any business. In 1999, as a tribute to parent Duke Energy's stellar performance, industry leaders voted it the most admired gas and electric company in *Fortune*'s annual poll.

The process-centered organization is both the end and the beginning of the reengineering road. A process-based organization is required to support and sustain the benefits of newly redesigned processes. That organization will provide the framework for future reengineering efforts. When processes are the central management theme of the organization, measuring and redesigning them is no longer an extraordinary event; it is a standard part of doing business. In a world of never-ending change, this may be the ultimate competitive advantage.

CHAPTER 11

ONE COMPANY'S EXPERIENCE: IBM

Few companies achieve the kind of industry preeminence and dominance that the International Business Machines Corporation (IBM), based in Armonk, New York, once commanded, then lost—and regained.

IBM's name was synonymous with computing. Its enormous investment in research and development left competitors in the dust. Its buttoned-down, striped-tie Big Blue sales force owned its territories. Even its blue-chip stock was considered a market bellwether.

The company possessed a distinguished record for making huge mainframes. In addition, IBM was the primary force behind the proliferation of the personal computer. In fact, its image was so powerful that when companies like Compaq and Dell began marketing PCs, the machines were known as IBM clones.

When its prominence in the PC market was challenged, big, unwieldy IBM, trapped by its starchy command-and-control hierarchy, could not move quickly enough to keep up with the changing PC market.

Sadly, by the early 1990s, IBM was no longer a company to emulate. It was cited in the press and used in business schools to exemplify how vast success could blind a company to its market realities.

When Louis V. Gerstner Jr. took over IBM in 1993, he found a company that was a shadow of its former self.

Just as few companies reach IBM's success, even fewer get a second chance to reclaim their former glory. But the Armonk legend has done just that.

IBM's profits are up, the stock price is soaring, and the company is once again cited as a model to emulate, not avoid. Lou Gerstner gets the well-deserved credit for this amazing turnaround. In this chapter, Jamie Hewitt, vice president of Business Process, explains how process reengineering helped IBM transform itself.

Until recently, many people thought of IBM as a large, bureaucratic, and unresponsive company. While our product lines were diverse and our market reach broad, we were unable to keep up with our newer and more streamlined competitors.

By 1993, we were in a real crisis. Our repeated attempts to stem the downturn included plans to break up IBM into smaller, more manageable units. But nothing had yielded the required results.

As a result of staggering losses and failed reengineering efforts, the Board of Directors brought in Lou Gerstner as chairman and chief executive officer.

He came from outside the company and had been an IBM customer himself. So his perspective was a little different from that of the people already inside. He was well aware of the increasing complexity of technology, and, additionally, he knew that what customers really needed and wanted was someone to pull all the fragmented pieces into a coherent whole for them. He recognized the power inherent in continuing as a single, integrated company.

Overall, most employees were relieved when Gerstner first came on board and announced that IBM was not breaking into smaller parts. But some people misunderstood, thinking that meant we would go back to operating in the old way.

That decision to change started us down a path that evolved into IBM's position today as a leader in the e-business revolution. In the process, we became very different from the IBM we were in 1993.

Gerstner and the senior leaders concentrated on two dimensions. First, they looked at near-term company operations. Simply put, we had to get our costs and cycle times down and our customer satisfaction up. We had to make it easier to do business with us.

Second, he determined that we needed to emphasize strategy more. In addition to the tactical maneuvers designed to bolster the balance sheet, we had to become a smarter, faster organization. We had to put all of our assets and knowledge toward making IBM—the enterprise—more competitive.

Becoming one IBM meant changing across many dimensions:

- From a country orientation to a customer segment and industry-based strategy
- From a hardware company to a diverse portfolio, including software services and technology
- From a predominantly internal sales force to one that embraced a wide array of channel partners
- From a product-based advertising to IBM as the brand

This new focus on operations and strategy generated a set of internal initiatives. First and foremost, common processes were established to run the company. Gerstner envisioned a team-based approach that relied on an information technology infrastructure for sharing and collaboration.

To launch these new initiatives, Gerstner took a number of actions:

- He assigned a senior executive to lead each reengineering effort. Given Gerstner's full proxy, these executives were responsible for executing the programs across the corporation.
- He established "Dear Colleague" letters to communicate important messages across IBM.
- He reviewed the results of each initiative quarterly and in key executive meetings.

Where once we had been very "country-centric," meaning IBM's operation in each country had its own redundant functions, Gerstner emphasized that each was an *IBM* company with shared characteristics. Sometimes, it is the small things that enable the organization to grasp the changes.

Rather than IBM France, IBM Germany, and so forth, the new thinking stressed IBM *in* France or IBM *in* Germany. In other words, we wanted everyone to envision a single corporate entity.

To translate this new way of thinking into practical applications, we reorganized our sales force with the goal of selling solutions to each industry. To this end, we

- Created a separate service team for each business, specifically to concentrate on growth.
- Reconfigured and reoriented our hardware, software, and technology teams so that they focused on groups of products, such as software or servers for office networks.
- Reoriented everyone's focus onto the customer, regardless of the immediate concern. This was the most significant change.
- Emphasized that supporting our externally facing teams were IBM Research, our common business processes, our shared information systems and applications, and our common management system.

That, in a nutshell, was our new go-to-market model.

IBM has a lot of practice with reorganization. In the distant past, reorganization was useful to communicate the company's focus, whereas in our most recent past, IT reorganizations had failed to solve our problem, so people felt skeptical that yet another reorganization effort would work.

This is where Gerstner's previous experience from outside of IBM served us particularly well. He had a lot of credibility with customers, and that, in turn, affected the way employees perceived his initiatives.

You see, many of our longtime customers had grown extremely frustrated with our poor response to their changing needs and problems. They thought we were cumbersome and sluggish—a lot like those antiquated, room-sized computers we used to build.

Gerstner could understand this, since he himself shared their experience. So customers listened when he talked about how he would change the company. Then, when they saw his promises become realities, they were quick to voice their delight.

As sales representatives started getting positive feedback, their skepticism about Gerstner's plans dissipated.

Line management made it clear that although we still had great products and great people, we were in trouble, and IT was necessary to make significant changes. For the plan to succeed, everyone had to see what Gerstner saw, so he led by example.

With his very direct, very human approach, he was able to get people fired up. He openly voiced his dismay at our defeats and our competitors' wins, feelings previously unstated at IBM. We had always been coached and counseled not to "lower yourself to the competition." Gerstner's way was a new kind of passionate leadership.

He changed the focus of his senior leadership group right away. Assigning responsibility for key parts of the business to members of his senior team, he held them accountable for driving whatever actions were required across IBM. They were responsible, too, for keeping the people involved thinking and working as a team. Decisions were made by the line management, not by a corporate committee.

Some people complained about this kind of matrix management structure. They thought it was too difficult. Gerstner required us to work outside formal lines of authority. He separated to whom we were responsible and accountable from direct control of all involved parties. In short, we had to learn new skills in teamwork and leadership that had not previously been evident in our DNA.

Gerstner is a straight shooter and he doesn't mince words. He reminded people who couldn't function in this way that there were other places to work.

At IBM, reengineering has been the mechanism for changing how we operate; that is, we have transformed the processes we use and the systems that support those processes into a more consistent, globally focused organization. It is a metamorphosis that encompasses our entire business.

We employed a holistic, structured approach that began when we defined our core business processes and assigned responsibility for them to top executives. First, we dismantled the processes to examine how they functioned and how competitive they were. Then, we used internal and external benchmarks to redesign them, deploy them, and provide the information technology systems to support them.

Once the new processes were in place, we measured them. We looked at how people's lives, behavior, or jobs had to change. This is a whole cycle: transform the process, build applications, run IT systems to support the new process, and then leverage the knowledge from these efforts to transform again. It is a circular, never-ending journey.

Actually, what we have done is, for the most part, straightforward, mainline reengineering. We created a fairly simple, easily understood process map focused on our major core processes: customer relationship management (CRM), integrated product development (IPD), integrated supply chain (ISC), and fulfillment. Encircling these are a number of supporting processes, such as human resources management, finance, and procurement.

We have been able to keep the same process map even though some things within the processes have changed and matured. That has been an advantage, since the map's simplicity makes it easy to understand and relate to the new model: suppliers on one side, customers on the other, and the processes that link them in between.

We initially identified eleven process initiatives across IBM. We have completed work on five of those, meaning they have undergone substantive transition and have achieved their original objectives. However, transformation never stops. We are now changing again based on an e-business model.

What happened with our hardware and software development exemplifies how process can unite a company. Initially, they began as two separate initiatives, but the teams soon realized that the differences between them were smaller than they originally thought. They combined and are now managed as a single process. In addition, this same process is now used for services offering development and transformational project management.

Some goals take longer to achieve than expected, and it is not unusual to rework something you thought was finished. We completed integrated product development in 1999 and integrated supply chain in 2000. Fulfillment and customer relationship management will be completed later than we first planned, probably in 2001.

One of the challenges with process-based management and reengineering is that what looks good on paper doesn't necessarily work in the real world. For example, we should have foreseen that customer relationship management needed a complete change in strategy. We didn't, and it slowed that team down.

They were focused strictly on helping badge-carrying IBM salespeople sell better. But, in fact, we now have 10,000 salespeople and 45,000 partners (distributors, resellers, etc.). Instead of squabbling over the much narrower issue of our own internal capabilities, we should have been taking a hard look at where our business was really going and how our processes should include our partners. Consequently, we have had to do a lot of retooling on that initiative.

Fulfillment has also been difficult. We decided to take a package-based approach using SAP. In addition to having limited experience with package-based transformation, we did not make the up-front business-based decision we should have. When problems and inconsistencies appeared during development and deployment, we had to debate them then and there, which stalled the whole process. Still, we learned valuable lessons.

It is obvious that we have experienced major changes in the past five or six years. A key to IBM's successful transformation, the thing that has promoted stability in our reengineering efforts, was Gerstner's decision to assign each process to one of the senior executives.

The way it works is that each process is owned by someone on the corporate executive committee. Some individuals own more than one process, but one process is not owned by more than one individual.

From the start, Gerstner made it very clear to these team members that they were personally accountable to themselves, to the corporation, and to their peers for developing and executing their assigned processes. Since all of those processes extend across units, the executives had to work together as a team. You can't do integrated supply-chain management, for example, just for one group. You have to work with each group: the personal systems group, the software group, and so on. The objectives apply to both the whole company and the specific group.

Having a management system that places accountability at the top of the business means that both strategic decisions and tactical problems get resolved quickly. If something can't be resolved between two executives, it is presented to the entire committee. But that seldom happens. In combination with the quarterly results inspection, the accountability system is a very powerful method of management.

Over the years, we've changed the way reengineering is handled within the company, and that is part of our story, too.

In the beginning, reengineering was a separate activity that reported to the chief financial officer at the corporate level. The group had its own budget, it focused on process design, and it was separated from the daily routine of the business. Many people involved in design teams came and went, depending on what stage the design was in and what skills were required at any particular moment.

When we began deploying the redesigned processes, we realized that reengineering needed to be integrated directly into the line business. Otherwise, you had folks from corporate handing a new process to the business leaders who had profit-and-loss responsibility but had not been involved in any aspect of the process's design. The person from corporate would explain to the leader how he or she would operate to enact the change, and that was not always helpful.

The line units had their own issues and priorities. Deploying new processes and supporting tools was often *not* at the top of their lists. In addition, even though the processes had been designed by teams that included people from their organizations, they frequently concluded that they wouldn't work for their specific group. Obviously, this resistance slowed down, if not occluded, deployment.

To remedy this situation, we kept the process teams intact, expanded their authority to include all IT spending, and moved them out of corporate into the line of the executive who was responsible for that process. For example, the executive responsible for the customer relationship management process is the global sales executive for all of IBM. The CRM reengineering team now reports to him and is now a part of his management system.

The corresponding change at the corporate level was to integrate IT and business into a single organization mirroring the alignment in the operating units.

In that milieu, the World Wide Web, information technology, and a company's processes are all intertwined in a way they have never been before. As we focused our efforts on IBM's transformation to an e-business, we have added responsibility for the Web to the BT/CIO office. We realized that companies above the "e-line" were seamlessly linking process, IT, and the Web. We were two-thirds of the way there, so it was easy to complete the picture and add Web responsibilities. The linking of process and IT is not particular to IBM. It is happening all over the industry.

During reengineering, you have to allow your management system to evolve as you move through the different phases of transformation. Everyone has to learn to be flexible, adaptive, and consistently prepared to change when obstacles are encountered.

For the most part, our management has done a good job of adjusting. It gets easier as we become increasingly able to reap the promised benefits from the initiatives. People become believers when they can see real business changes for themselves.

Problems still crop up, of course. We still churn on decisions far too long—partly because we're driven by the belief that we can arrive at the one "right" answer. It's classic analysis paralysis. It's important to recognize that there are often multiple answers—you just have to pick one.

Another element we include within our reengineering efforts is a consistent approach to setting objectives, evaluating ourselves, getting paid, and so forth. A key part of our reengineered human resource process, we call this approach "personal business commitments," and it works in cascade fashion.

Once a year, the chairman defines his commitments using a common framework that touches on three areas: win, execute, and team. He sends his objectives to the executives who report directly to him.

They, in turn, further define these objectives in relation to their specific responsibilities, including how to measure success. All of this cascades down to their teams and throughout the corporation.

In January, all employees of the corporation are assessed according to how closely they came to meeting their goals, and they are paid based on how their unit performed as a whole. Considered in scoring a unit's performance is how well it did fulfilling a set of previously stated reengineering objectives.

There is no guesswork or subjectivity involved in deciding these rewards. They are based on subjective measures. It is a clear system in which assessments are tied to business results as well as to process metrics.

The pool of money available to a particular unit, what we call "variable pay," can increase or decrease based on a set of corporatewide objectives, including reengineering objectives. An individual's variable pay is calculated based on his or her individual performance within the overall performance of their group. We have raised the bar on variable pay, thereby rewarding employees for the results IBM, as a whole, achieves. In short, we are giving them a direct stake in IBM's success.

We saw a quantum leap in attention, interest, and involvement when we linked compensation to the attainment of reengineering objectives.

Yet that's only one of the things we've done to make reengineering real to people. I believe that ownership and involvement have evolved to the point that reengineering is a compelling issue at all levels of the organization.

Each year, for example, the Chairman's Award is given to one or two teams that have demonstrated excellence in customer relations and have contributed the most to improving business operations. Typically, it goes to teams that interface directly with customers. But in 1999, the award went to our procurement process team for their tremendous success in reshaping procurement into an e-business.

Taking up Gerstner's challenge to turn IBM into the world's premier e-business, this team set its sights on becoming the best e-business within IBM. And their results were fabulous.

Purchase-order processing time went from one month to one day. The time it takes to get a contract in place dropped from six to twelve months to one month. Average contract length shrank from forty pages to six. The team completely transformed the procurement process, which had been paper-oriented and very local with no economies of scale or ability to negotiate.

Most interesting to people who understand procurement is the drop in our rate of maverick buying—down to less than 2 percent from 30 percent. Because maverick buying occurs, by definition, outside the process, it means bad terms, poor conditions, and no quantity discounts. We estimated that $6 billion a year was acquired "outside" the process, but not any more.

As an additional reward, more than 85 percent of IBMers now say they are satisfied with the procurement process, when only 40 percent were before. Internal satisfaction is a key test of process team success, so this is a superb accomplishment.

A critical realization for us during this endeavor was that, like anything else, reengineering needs to be executed with discipline. You set objectives, establish milestones, then measure yourself against those milestones. It is no different from bringing a product to market, and it must be taken just as seriously. In fact, we use the same process to manage reengineering as we use for product development.

For the process to benefit your business, you must try to predict various project management scenarios in their entirety.

Look at reengineering in a holistic way. It includes the process, the IT system that supports it, the organizations that use it, and the culture of your corporation. Each facet is inextricably entwined with the others, and all must be managed within a single project, within a single time frame. If you try to manage only one element at a time, you will fail because they are interdependent.

Probably the single most significant lesson we learned is that you can never underestimate the need for constant communication. Saying something once is usually insufficient; just because you said it certainly does not mean everyone has heard you. You have to continuously repeat yourself and find different ways to convey your message so that it reaches different groups of people.

Certainly, there have been dramatic changes at IBM, and I would be remiss if I didn't talk about how reengineering has affected jobs and organizational structure.

First of all, the organization has definitely become flatter, because as we reorganized to compete in a global environment, we made our sales force much more mobile. We removed layers from our structure, and by definition, layoffs ensued. Our workforce plummeted to 285,000, from 400,000 in the early 90s.

Not all of the shrinkage was directly attributable to reengineering. Considering the money-losing situation we were in in the early 1990s, we would have taken some of these actions anyway. But reengineering allowed us to keep going because people were now more autonomous and know what to do without a manager to guide them every step of the way. This, in turn, freed managers to devote more time to business issues.

In one sense, we had something of a chicken-or-egg situation. Because reengineering is a streamlining process, you can afford to redirect or cut back the workforce. Therefore, one could argue that since we had to lay off people anyway, we were even more eager to reengineer our processes.

From a cultural standpoint, probably the biggest shift has been the move to a collaborative environment. We were not a team-based culture before Gerstner became CEO. Individual excellence was the battle cry at IBM. Gerstner prodded us to share information, share both successes and failures. Still, were it not for the commonality of processes and infrastructure brought about by reengineering, collaboration would have been impossible.

A prime example of the benefits of consistency wrought by reengineering processes can be seen in our human resources department. We now have job-family descriptions defined in the same terms all around the world. Before we were virtually talking in tongues, but now people from different departments can compare their résumés and skill levels and know they are speaking the same language.

Ironically, it has taken us much longer to complete process reengineering than we had anticipated, yet we have realized far more benefits from it than we imagined we would. Starting out, we couldn't completely comprehend what was involved or what it would yield long term. While we had hopes and expectations, we needed actual positive results in order to accelerate our efforts.

I would advise anyone considering a reengineering program to confront early on the tough business decisions that such a transformation demands. Don't assume that problems will get swept under the carpet or that somebody lower in the organization will make decisions for you. This "reengineering thing" will not just happen. You have to vigorously attack the business issues and then actively demonstrate leadership from the top down. We lost time not realizing these important matters soon enough.

Though we have not finished phase 1 in all areas, IBM has already entered what I would call phase 2, which is to make IBM itself operate as an e-business.

While our groups work on *what* we sell, our efforts focus on *how* we work. Having gone down this path before, we know how to avoid known pitfalls and, hopefully, how to quickly address new ones. We intend to take full advantage of the lessons we learned the first time around.

Everyone knows that IBM has executed one of the most dramatic turnarounds in modern business history. As Jamie Hewitt informs us, much of the credit for the company's renaissance can be traced to its passionate embrace of reengineering. Strategy and vision are crucial, but without new ways of doing business, they are just pieces of paper.

In fact, the reengineering program that Jamie describes was IBM's second effort. In the early 1990s, it was one of the first corporations to undertake reengineering. We personally gave seminars on the topic to hundreds of IBM personnel and taught them many of the techniques that they would later successfully employ.

But IBM's first generation of reengineering efforts went nowhere. Design teams were convened, existing processes were studied, new ideas were developed, but no real changes were ever made. Why not? And why was the company's second round, four years later, so successful? In a word, leadership: It starts at the top. The ability to sustain transformation can only happen when all the leaders embrace it.

It is a commonplace, perhaps even a cliché: Major change cannot succeed unless it is driven by a passionate executive leader. IBM's first efforts never got off the ground because they were crushed by the company's legendary bureaucracy. Without strong commitment from the top, change programs end with a whimper, not a bang. At IBM, as well as at many other companies involved in reengineering, we see symptoms of an organization whose management structure is fiercely resisting the effort toward change, but never actually admits its opposition. The symptoms include struggles to protect turf that masquerade as substantive debates; endless arguments about authority; and resources assigned and then taken away.

Gerstner and his senior leaders changed all that. He articulated a new strategic vision for IBM: a company that would satisfy customers' needs by operating with common processes around the world, thereby avoiding the balkanization that results when each country or product group devises its own way of working. Gerstner made changes in the company's structure and, when necessary, in its leadership team so that it aligned with this vision. At the same time, he made a major commitment to reengineering as the vehicle the company would employ for creating new processes for the new IBM.

With his formidable communication skills, Lou Gerstner proselytized for his vision, convincing all levels at IBM that these changes were absolutely necessary and that he was committed to seeing them through. Once this commitment was made, he brooked no opposition. Those employees who did not see the virtues of common processes were reminded that they could look for work elsewhere. He built support for reengineering into IBM's management systems, first by assigning personal responsibility for each process to a very senior executive and then by linking people's rewards to process performance. With this level of passion and commitment, perhaps it is not surprising that IBM's second wave of reengineering has been spectacularly successful.

In addition to the lesson about the power of leadership, we can glean other important insights from Jamie's account. One worth repeating is that reengineering has to be undertaken in a disciplined fashion. IBM developed a methodology for understanding, redesigning, and implementing its processes and deployed this methodology across the company.

Another is that reengineering was not managed as a stand-alone activity. It was tightly integrated with information systems management, since technology is the essential enabler of new processes.

Yet another lesson is that, like true love, the course of reengineering never runs smooth. As Jamie says, "What looks good on paper doesn't necessarily work in the real world." You must expect to make mistakes and be prepared to go back and try things again. At IBM, even the list of the company's processes evolved over time, as people developed deeper insights into process thinking.

One more insight is that reengineering has to be made part of line management's responsibility. A central reengineering group can have authority over technique and offer a pool of reengineering talent, but the line managers must be held accountable for improved process results, otherwise, the effort will deteriorate into recriminations and finger-pointing.

IBM has been extremely successful with reengineering, but they are not resting on their laurels. Right now they are going back to rethink, yet again, many of their processes that they thought were finished. Why? Because of the Internet. Lou Gerstner has layered another level of vision and strategy onto his existing one. If IBM is to offer e-business tools and services, then it must be an e-business itself. Still, even after reengineering, most of the company's processes were not ready for the Web. Now they are working again and, undoubtedly, not for the last time. Neither Lou Gerstner nor anyone else at IBM wants to come as close to the edge as the company did in the early 1990s. Reengineering is here to stay at IBM as the basis for growth and leadership in an e-world.

CHAPTER 12

ONE COMPANY'S EXPERIENCE: DEERE

Deere & Company, of Moline, Illinois, is a company whose history is closely linked to the triumphs and struggles of the agricultural industry in the midwestern United States over the past 150 years.

Founded by blacksmith John Deere in the mid-1800s and incorporated as Deere & Company in 1868, the company first achieved prominence on the strength of the self-scouring steel plow, a design that allowed farmers to successfully till the uncommonly rich Midwest soil. From that beginning, Deere grew into the world's largest producer of agricultural machinery, and a top maker of construction and lawn-care equipment as well.

In 1998, Deere saw sales rise 8 percent to more than $13 billion, even though the nation's heartland struggled to survive depressed grain and livestock prices. The company's successful diversification efforts receive the credit. (As the head of Deere's commercial and consumer equipment division told *Forbes*, "Grass has to get cut whether soybean prices are up or down.")

Still, growth in the midst of turmoil has not always been Deere's experience. The company suffered during a bout of economic distress in the mid-1980s, although it emerged healthier. But when hard times struck the farm sector again at the beginning of the 1990s,

Deere's sales and profits were beaten down like a Kansas wheat field after an early-summer hailstorm. It was a most unwelcome turn of events for the company's new chairman and chief executive officer, Hans W. Becherer, who took over in 1990.

At this time, Deere embarked on a reengineering initiative. Although the terminology was new, Deere was no stranger to this kind of change, having undergone a major overhaul in its manufacturing operations a decade before. However, this time it was beginning an effort that would eventually touch nearly every corner of the venerable manufacturer's operations. "Reengineering changes all aspects of how you do business," observes Gary Gesme, a veteran of Deere's change programs. In fact, Gesme believes that reengineering has transformed Deere into a resilient company that will be more able to withstand the cyclical downturns that have troubled it in the past.

Gesme was an important catalyst of the early reengineering efforts, and he remains involved as director of job process and information in Deere's construction equipment division. In the pages that follow, he and Max Guinn, who was on staff during the early reengineering of the Deere manufacturing operation in Dubuque, Iowa, discuss their experiences and what business process reengineering has meant for the company.

Gesme: Back in the early 1980s, the Midwest was becoming known as the Rust Belt, and manufacturing was under extreme pressure. It was a do-or-die situation. Manufacturing just had to improve its ability to compete.

At Deere, we embarked on a program of radical change that later became known as reengineering. Our first efforts centered on improving manufacturing processes on the shop floor. We eliminated material movement, work in process, and inventories. We formed a hierarchy of process centers instead—what we called manufacturing cells, manufacturing modules, and focused factories.

Cells came first. The idea was to group similar pieces of a process together and have one operator make an entire part. Modules emerged after that. We rearranged the shop floor so that cells that were to be built up into the same subassembly were grouped next to each other in a module. From there, it was easy to group the modules together to create a factory inside the factory, which eliminated large amounts of work-in-process inventory and put the work in the hands of self-directed teams.

If you stood on a mezzanine overlooking the shop floor in 1980, you would have seen a huge mass of machine tools and forklifts moving materials around in all directions. And a station operator would perform the same operation—maybe fabricating, or drilling, or bending a certain part—from the time he started in the morning until quitting time at night.

Now if you look down on the shop floor, you will see a radically different situation. It looks like there's nothing going on because there's no movement, no forklifts rolling all over the place anymore. People use several machines to make a whole part. And after a person finishes building a part, it's moved across the aisle and into one of four or five modules that are sequenced along an assembly line. Sure, there are still some machines moving down through the line, but the level of activity on the shop floor is much less than it was in 1980.

Throughout the 1980s, Deere was doing this kind of reengineering on the shop floor, but the "R" word hadn't been invented yet. Our connection to Michael Hammer began after we heard him speak in San Francisco in the fall of 1989. Subsequently, in 1990, the company kicked off its first commitment to what by then was known as reengineering.

Basically, the idea was to take some of the concepts we had learned on the shop floor and try to apply them to our business processes. It was damn hard, too, despite the company's previous experience with significant change. In fact, our first attempt failed miserably.

Four of us were asked to head up this new initiative, which began in April 1991. We spent the early months just trying to figure out if reengineering had a hyphen in it or not! We didn't know how to get started, so that first summer we lived at our dealerships, trying to get connected to our customers. We knew we had to understand our customers better. Late in the summer, we went to one of Michael's first classes. And in the fall, feeling that we at least had a sense of what we needed to attack, we began our first reengineering project at Deere.

The mistake we made was focusing on too big a project at the start—the center of our business, the order fulfillment process in the agriculture division. In retrospect, we probably also went in with a plan that had too little detail. The redesign was too conceptual, which opened the door to a "it's not broken, so why try to fix it?" response. But there were also just too many years of history built up in the agriculture division, the culture was too entrenched, and people were afraid of change of that magnitude. We tried to deal with the fear, but eventually we ended up putting that project on hold.

At the time, Deere was structured into eight divisions, all managed very separately. So we decided to ask the various divisions to invite us in to do reengineering if they were interested. We let them come to us instead of trying to force change from the outside. Suddenly, invitations from the various divisions started to flow in.

There is a theory that paradigms break through on the fringe of your business before they reach the center. That proved to be very true in our situation. Our first invitation came from our insurance business, which is not one of our primary operations, and that was followed by interest from our operation in Mexico, the one in Australia, and from our lawn and garden division. Gradually, the reengineering effort was spiraling toward the core of our business in the agricultural division.

We learned that it's best to start small, at the edges of your business. You've got to get results, of course, and then that success attracts more interest. Each of our reengineering projects led to another invitation. But you also have to realize that some reengineering projects are going to be more successful than others, and some might not work at all for a variety of reasons.

The first reengineering project to get off the ground was for John Deere Insurance, which wrote commercial lines of insurance to dealerships—John Deere equipment dealers, auto dealers, boat dealers, recreational vehicle dealers. That division needed to redesign its claims and quoting processes for contracts in order to reduce cycle time and cut down on the number of people who handled a piece of paper.

When a request from the field came in, it was put in a folder with a bar code. Then it started to make its rounds through the building so everybody could perform his or her specialty on it. Some thirty days later, out came a final quote. The situation was an exact analogy to what we had faced on the shop floor, except that the insurance employees weren't grinding and drilling holes. They were performing underwriting activities to assess the risk on quotes for the dealerships.

By forming case teams, John Deere Insurance was able to reduce the turnaround time rather significantly—40 percent of the elapsed time was eliminated. When computerization was added, the time period for turning out a final quote was cut by another 40 percent.

Word spread about the successful changes in the insurance business, and other people jumped on the bandwagon. The head of the Mexican operation asked us in 1992 to reengineer several processes there. He became committed to reengineering after sitting down and talking with the president of John Deere Insurance, but he wanted us to convince his organization that it was the right thing to do. So we went down to

Mexico and spent a day taking the employees through what was called "a leadership process of understanding."

At the Mexico operation, we reengineered the order fulfillment processes for implements and for tractors. After that, we trained a few people on how to do this thing called reengineering. They then set up their own program and basically became self-sustaining down there.

Our reengineering group was small, six or seven people, but we became a corporate department, if you will, in 1993. We sent people to all of Michael's classes, and also had some in-house classes and workshops for them two or three times a year. We were acting as enablers, going out and working with project teams in the business. Demand for reengineering was very high by then.

I would go out in the field to visit with the teams and work with the leadership group. Every reengineering project had an owner, a leadership steering committee, and a project team of twelve to fifteen people who spanned the breadth of the process being reengineered.

We went through about fifteen to twenty-five projects, and they kept getting bigger and bigger. Soon we got our first chance to really connect with some of our major factories from a process context, not a shop floor context. It got into the issue of what we call "make the order" for order fulfillment.

Our first major breakthrough in that area occurred in our Dubuque, Iowa, factory, which builds construction equipment—the yellow equipment you see at construction sites and on road projects. The breakthrough was driven by the general manager, Mike Triplett, who took on two projects.

One involved reengineering the process of order fulfillment from the time the factory received the order until it shipped. The other involved reengineering product development from the point of concept commitment to the first production shipment. As a result of these projects the shop floor was rearranged, order fulfillment teams were created and located next to the assembly lines, product development was split in two, and a portion of that activity was merged with the order fulfillment team. Both reengineering projects were very successful. In fact, we even took the chairman out there to see results—it was that far-reaching.

Guinn: I worked for Mike Triplett at the Dubuque facility in 1993, which some people consider to be the start of the reengineering effort there. It's important to understand that we were not really focused on reengineering. We were focused on improving the business. We viewed reengineering as one of the tools that would help us achieve that outcome.

We'd had a quality focus for a long time. Suddenly it dawned on us that the issue of quality involved much more than our products—things like the quality of our workplace and the quality of our service were also important. That led us to thinking about how we could take some tools from the product quality world and apply them to the business world.

In reengineering terms, the first step is to map the process, because you can't improve anything if you can't define it. We came to the conclusion that we needed to map the management process. We ended up identifying what we affectionately called the "leadership process," which was a process map to describe how our organization undertakes the leadership function. That was very powerful for us.

Simultaneously, we had reengineering projects going in order fulfillment and product delivery. But we didn't really understand how those things fit together until we started to think about our own jobs differently. We came to see that, as management, we have a constant role of evaluating the environment we work in and the way in which we compete in that environment. We also have a responsibility to communicate our strategic intent and our vision to the organization.

So mapping the leadership process allowed us to look at the management as a process. It kept us focused on our responsibilities as a leadership group and gave us a mechanism to communicate the organization's most important initiatives and launch them as improvement activities.

At the time, I was head of supply management, and using the more disciplined approach made me realize that the supply management function by itself has very little value inside the organization. It is really just an enabler for the order fulfillment process and the product delivery process, two areas where our customers have distinct requirements and recognize our performance.

Bingo! Customers, I realized, don't care about functions or specific activities that occur within our organization. The end game is whether they are getting the right product at the right time at a competitive price.

So the leadership process idea led to stripping away the classic suboptimization that occurs when one person tries to be the best at supply management while another is trying to be the best at improving product quality.

As for product delivery, we developed our first process in that area in 1994. That was the first time we really sat down and looked at product delivery as a process defined and chartered to deliver a product to a customer—something of a revolutionary idea for us in that it led us to focus on colocation and cross-functional teaming. Previously, product delivery was viewed merely as a result of a series of specific actions that take place in engineering, supply management, and manufacturing.

Before reengineering, we had a long string of product introductions that ended up being successful, but often had problems at launch—behind schedule, above cost, unreliable performance. Since reengineering, there have been vast improvements. For example, our latest significant new product at Dubuque was twice as reliable at introduction as the one it replaced. And production costs were cut by about 10 percent.

We've probably made the most progress—and probably still have the furthest to go—in the area of supplier integration. The analysis of the product delivery process (PDP) helped people to focus on the importance of treating suppliers as an extension of our factory, not just as people who supply us with material. Defining a PDP on paper drove home the fact that people designing a component in a facility 500 miles away or halfway around the world really had the same impact on our customer as the people sitting right here in Dubuque.

The early work in the construction division clearly illustrated the power of process. The division president made commitments to use process to transform the division and enable the customer connection. Anchoring the beginning and end of a process with a customer enabled a customer focus strategy. A director was put in place to help with the transformation.

The first divisionwide process was order fulfillment. It was developed as a divisionwide process after experiencing some of the early results of reengineering. The success was a direct result of the commitment and leadership of the president. We believe the change will halve our total order fulfillment time. We call it the estimate-to-cash process, which, as we define it, starts when a dealer estimates a product requirement based on a customer's input and runs until the dealer gets paid for the product. That, we believe, is an all-inclusive definition of order fulfillment.

Back in 1993 or 1994, when we did our first order fulfillment process reengineering, we defined the process as running from receipt of a dealer's order until the order was shipped. Compared to today's estimate-to-cash process, the old definition actually represents a very small portion of the order fulfillment cycle. And to me, that change illustrates some learning within the organization about the importance of focusing on customer needs, as opposed to internal or functional needs.

As I said earlier, though, mapping the leadership process itself was very powerful for us. The key to success with the order fulfillment and the PDP projects was applying reengineering at the right level of the organization. That's why seeing leadership as a process was such a big deal for us. It wasn't just changing a process. It was a transformation.

Gesme: The Dubuque project really created some stir at the topmost levels of Deere. As part of the snowball effect, the agriculture division came back and asked us to take a look at the tillage products of their business. These are the tools that you pull behind the tractor to turn the dirt and prepare the seed bed for planting.

Although the agriculture business had no national competitor that built tillage equipment like we did, it was facing about seventy regional competitors around the country. It had been struggling to improve its business but wasn't doing very well. We really walked into a critical situation and had to try to figure out how to maintain that business. The one positive in a situation like that, though, is that everybody is ready to change.

The thing you have to understand is that involvement of leadership is key to the success of these projects. In addition, a reengineering initiative has to be given enough dedicated resources. Part-time teams won't be able to develop the breakthroughs you need to improve performance.

But regardless of the level of commitment from the upper echelon or the acquisition of dedicated resources, there is always going to be some resistance somewhere to the idea of change. And the most challenging thing to deal with is resistance from employees. As we said, resistance forced us to scuttle our first effort in the agriculture division.

On the other hand, the Mexico operation was one that offered little resistance. That's probably because it was pretty fresh, with many new employees. That means people haven't been in their jobs as long as they have in other parts of the company. We're finding that it's the length of time in a particular job, not the age of the person or even total years of service, this seems to create the most resistance.

People get into a rhythm that makes them resistant to change. To understand the mind-set, try switching hands when you brush your teeth in the morning. It's extremely difficult.

Guinn: In Dubuque, we experienced the most resistance in some of the functional areas like engineering. We've had, and continue to have, challenges getting people to remember that we're working on processes, not functions. Of course, there are also individuals in our organization who really don't want to do anything different and don't want to see a bigger picture.

I'm not criticizing them for that. They're not pushing back on purpose. It's the way we trained people for thirty years—to be focused on optimizing an activity instead of a process. The retraining effort was, and continues to be, significant.

Gesme: The whole idea of change brings up the issue of fear. People resist because they're fearful. Of late, we've been trying to do more work with what we call "change leadership." It's all designed to eliminate fear.

An example occurred when we implemented our biggest project to date, the estimate-to-cash process, in the construction division in November 1998. We've never defined order fulfillment so broadly before. That reengineering project took a total of nineteen months from diagnosis through national implementation, which was breakneck speed for change in a company as complex as Deere.

In order to counter resistance and fear, the division president, Pierre Leroy, who was committed to redesigning the process, finally had to decide for the division that this had to be done. Other leaders in the division said this had been done before. Therefore it had to be made part of their individual performance goals.

To counter resistance with employees and dealers, we did things like creating a Monopoly-type board game in which equipment dealers played "order fulfillment."

We sat eight to ten dealers down to play the game together. After playing for about forty-five minutes, they began to realize that the new estimate-to-cash process wasn't going to be very hard after all. Certain things had to be done on the twentieth of the month, something else at the end of the month. Experiencing the estimate-to-cash process in a two-hour game context took away the dealers' fears. The whole idea was to have fun and get rid of any anxiety over what this process change was going to mean in a day-to-day business situation.

Believe me, it required a lot of planning. We aren't used to doing this sort of thing at Deere—we build tractors! But we wanted to get the correct information out in a fun way.

Something else we did was buy this little apparatus from a consulting company called an RQ, or resistance quotient. We actually call it an AQ, for "acceptance quotient." It consists of a handheld transmitter and a receiver on a personal computer that is connected to a screen.

We designed questions and brought in employee groups of thirty, forty, no more than fifty people, randomly chosen from a process. When we asked a question, they responded by dialing in a number on the transmitter to represent a range of positive or negative feelings. The responses were blind, so people could feel free to express their true opinions. We needed to know exactly where the group stood so that we could move to counteract any resistance with information and education.

We tailored our whole communication strategy based on the findings. We knew which groups were getting the message and which weren't. The shop floor? The middle managers?

Who was and who wasn't connecting to the reengineering project?

Some resistance to reengineering developed as a result of articles in the press. In fact, around 1995 we renamed it "business transformation," in part because the "R" word had taken on a lot of negative connotations. The press didn't understand reengineering and had connected it with downsizing. But it wasn't about eliminating people. It was about changing the way you work. We had done a lot of process reengineering since 1991, but we hadn't downsized.

At John Deere Insurance, we needed to reduce staff, but since we had a natural turnover of about 15 percent a year, we used attrition to bring staff size down to the required level.

There have been a variety of other scenarios. We have reassigned people because of reengineering. We've had some special programs, such as voluntary early retirement. In one case, we actually did some reengineering in order to deal with a staff reduction brought on by an early retirement program. But I don't believe that anyone has left the company directly as a result of business process reengineering.

Guinn: One of the key ways to break down resistance and spread the message—and I think Gary hit on it earlier—is to start small and be successful. One key to getting things to catch fire here was having a successful team early on and then publicizing that success, letting people know about desired behavior and desirable outcomes.

That early order fulfillment project was a part of that, as was PDP. Even some of the subprocesses within those major processes were opportunities to demonstrate success and get a couple of fast starts.

Not everything went right, of course, and we made tons of mistakes along the way. We reengineered as a factory whereas I think we should have done it as a business. I would try to instill this type of thinking into an entire business or business unit, as opposed to a geographic area of the business or one particular site. That would involve manufacturing and marketing going through this transition at the same time, together.

Gesme: We went through the early times by the seat of our pants in some cases. Sure, we were successful in the sense that it took less time to get results. That is usually what occurs because reengineering eliminates all the extra processing that you just don't need to do.

But beyond that, we did not do a good job of tracking our improvements. We never had a good control group on the front side and back side of a change. It was so logical that there was never any hesitation going forward. But once you make the step forward, if you don't have earlier measurements, you can't do a comparison. Having some kind of scorecard as we went along might have accelerated succeeding projects. Maybe we could have done in two years what took four, or done in four years what took eight.

We also should have gotten senior management involved earlier. We should have made reengineering a part of the management fabric sooner. As it was, we didn't pass that milestone until 1997.

In the fall of 1996 and the first part of 1997, we approached the chairman and suggested that reengineering should be done as part of our overall business management strategy, not just in the context of a project or an event. He agreed. So in early 1997 Deere decided to merge business transformation with efforts going on in the quality area, total quality management and such.

We put together a team of ten people from around the company to look at all areas where we were doing process improvement—from rapid projects on the shop floor that take five days to multiyear projects focused on an entire business process. We tried to come up with a methodology that was scalable across the enterprise and applicable to any aspect of the business. We spent the whole summer, about ten to twelve weeks, doing this. We did benchmark visits with AlliedSignal and General Electric.

What emerged was a concept we call Aim, which is the leadership piece, and Impact, which is the process redesign piece. Whether Aim and Impact are being applied to a small part of a business or a large part, you follow the same process. The methodology was adopted under the designation business process excellence (BPE) and was rolled out on an enterprise-wide basis by our chairman in December 1997.

Now our annual report talks about process redesign in a major way, and we have a BPE center in Moline that deals with the issue of training and education. We've designed a job description for a "process pro," who is an on-site catalyst, leader, or enabler for a project team. We also have a few "master process pros" in each of our divisions.

Since BPE was adopted as part of the fabric of corporate management strategy, projects go even faster because employees are aware that this is the way we do business. We're a cyclical company, but our commitment to shareholders is to never lose money, even in our deepest trough. We're working hard at fulfilling that promise, and business process reengineering has helped by making us a tougher, more resilient company.

As for the future, obviously we are committed to reengineering. There are a lot of projects going on—a whole lineup from small to large. The question is whether or not we can go to enterprise-level processes and maintain the breakthroughs we've come to enjoy. Previously, we've put together twelve- to fifteen-member teams that were able to create process breakthroughs at the division level. But working at the enterprise level implies large groups, say, thirty or more people, and the chemistry of large groups is such that solutions are usually designed to accommodate the lowest common denominator. Aggressive, breakthrough-type solutions tend to get squelched. We're working on overcoming the group psychology problem.

The thing about reengineering is that it changes all aspects of how you do business. So it doesn't seem to make any difference where you stand, because wherever you are, you're at the edge, and at the edge you can see how much more there is to do. The edge just keeps moving out there on you. The more you learn, the more you realize how much there is to do. That continues for us even today.

Guinn: That's right. We used to sit around and think, "Boy, once we get this order fulfillment system in, and once we get the latest investments done for the new piece of equipment that we're putting into production, then things will stabilize for a little while."

I see now that that's never going to happen. I don't think you ever stop. At the Dubuque works, we have another PDP reengineering team working right now on development of a new generation of PDP. We're installing our latest order fulfillment system, and we're already talking about how we can change it to make it better.

I think these activities help people understand that change and improvement will go on forever. There isn't an end to it, so you've got to get comfortable with that—and, to a large extent, this organization has become comfortable with change.

You can celebrate accomplishments, but after a while, you need to start celebrating the speed at which you're traveling instead of the destination you've reached. I think we're getting there.

For many companies, perhaps most, reengineering is high drama. Organizations undertake it for an assortment of reasons. Some resort to it when they hit the brink of disaster and discover that their ways of conducting business have grown so complex and their overhead so high that they can no longer profitably meet customer needs. Others encounter a fundamental shift in their marketplaces, caused by a technological innovation, sudden changes in customer requirements, deregulation, or the advent of a new class of competitors. Still others are led into reengineering by a senior executive who, for lack of a better phrase, has a religious experience, seeing in a blinding flash of light the power of process transformation. In such cases, reengineering represents a clean break with the company's past. The slate is wiped clean and the organization completely reinvents how it operates.

This dramatic school of reengineering has certain advantages. It does make the decision to undertake reengineering easier for executives to reach and easier for employees to accept. But there is another path to reengineering, one more evolutionary than revolutionary, which builds upon a company's history rather than departs from it. If IBM is a striking case of the dramatic approach, John Deere illustrates a gentler alternative.

Deere is a venerable company with a proud tradition. Indeed, the company name is practically synonymous with agricultural equipment. When Deere decided to reengineer, it was still successful and profitable. But Gary Gesme and some of his colleagues were farsighted and understood the power of reengineering. They felt there must be better ways of operating at Deere. Theirs was not a frontal assault on the company and its processes, however. Rather, it was more of a guerrilla campaign. Reengineering at Deere wasn't introduced as an alien concept to be imposed from the outside. It was posed as a natural outgrowth of the company's long-standing commitment to improvement and to its highly regarded quality program.

Early on, Gary and his colleagues made a misstep. They attempted to reengineer the core process of order fulfillment before the organization was ready. Wisely, they retreated and began to build support by creating reengineering successes in areas where the stakes were lower: the shop floor, the insurance unit, and operations in Mexico. These segments of Deere, which were less entrenched in their old ways of doing business, viewed reengineering as an extension of work they were already performing, and they had little trouble accepting it. Successes here were then used to gain support from the organization as a whole, but especially from senior management.

Nonetheless, the techniques of reengineering and their accompanying behaviors were unfamiliar territory at Deere. For one thing, as Gary succinctly reminds us, they "build tractors." For another, decades of ingrained functional behavior is not easily undone. The reengineering team gave change management the concerted attention and creativity it deserves. They did all of the following: They listened to people to make sure they understood and could accurately address people's concerns and feelings. They employed board games to diminish anxiety and help people understand the need for change. And they managed a relentless communication program. In other words, they used all the tools in the change management arsenal, and ultimately their efforts paid off. Reengineering was applied to the company's core processes with great success.

Throughout, Deere never lost track of its goal. As Max Guinn says, "We were focused on improving the business," not ideologically committed to reengineering as a doctrine. When the term "reengineering" acquired some negative connotations, they used a different term: "business transformation." Eventually, reengineering was subsumed into an even larger endeavor: an overarching change initiative entitled process excellence that now serves as an umbrella for a number of other efforts as well.

This is extremely important. Too many companies have too many uncoordinated change initiatives, which lead to confusion and paralysis. Rather than wasting energy on looking for boundaries between, say, reengineering and quality improvement, Deere has brought them all together under process excellence.

Deere has managed to institutionalize reengineering. It is no longer a project with a completion date, but a way of life. The company has recognized that things will never settle down, that change is here to stay, and that an ongoing commitment to reengineering—by any name—is the only way to survive.

CHAPTER 13

SUCCEEDING AT REENGINEERING

Sadly, we must report that despite the success stories described in previous chapters, many companies that begin reengineering don't succeed at it. They end their efforts precisely where they began, making no significant changes, achieving no major performance improvement, and fueling employee cynicism with yet another ineffective business improvement program. Our unscientific estimate is that as many as 50 to 70 percent of the organizations that undertake a reengineering effort do not achieve the dramatic results they intended.

Nonetheless, while we say reengineering is often unsuccessful, it is not a high-risk endeavor. This apparent oxymoron isn't oxymoronic at all. Consider the difference in risk between roulette and chess. Roulette is a high-risk endeavor; chess is not, although a player may lose at chess as frequently as at roulette. Roulette is purely a game of chance. Once the money is put down, players have no control over the outcome; in chess, chance plays no part in the outcome. The better player can expect to win; loss results from ability and strategy.

As with chess, so with reengineering: The key to success lies in knowledge and ability, not in luck. If you know the rules and avoid making mistakes, you're extremely likely to succeed. In reengineering, moreover, the same mistakes get made over and over. The first step to reengineering success, therefore, is to recognize these common failures and learn to avoid them.

The Russian chess champion Sergei Tartakower once said of a chess board that was set up for a game, "The mistakes are all there, waiting to be made." What follows is a catalog of the most common errors that lead companies to fail at reengineering. Avoid them, and you almost can't help but get it right.

• Try to fix a process instead of changing it

The most egregious way to fail at reengineering is by not reengineering at all, but rather conducting process changes and just calling it reengineering. The term "reengineering" has acquired a certain cachet, and it has been attached to all kinds of programs that in fact have nothing to do with radical process redesign. We find it useful to recall the old saying that hanging a sign on a cow that says "I am a horse" doesn't make it a horse.

We described in Chapter 2 how IBM Credit Corporation reengineered its credit issuance process. However, we neglected to say that IBM Credit first tried to "fix" the old process several times before it faced up to the need for radical process redesign.

The company first attempted to automate the existing process, using computer technology to speed up the information flows and task performance. Automation consisted of giving the specialists on-line computer terminals into which they could type the results of their individual efforts. They still did their work on their respective departments' own off-line computers, and each deal was still handled serially—first by credit, then by business practices, then by pricing, and so on. The paper application forms continued to travel from department to department. In fact, the only benefit that this automation brought to IBM Credit was that it enabled the specialists who performed the final step (quote letter preparation) to extract the results of the previous steps of the process from the on-line system. In trying to automate its operations, IBM Credit managed only to immortalize a bad process by committing it to computer software, making it even more difficult to alter in the future.

Dissatisfied with the paltry performance improvement obtained from automation, the company next attempted a whole stable of business improvement techniques. It tried using queuing theory and linear programming techniques to balance the work across the various departments to minimize wait times. The results proved insignificant. The company set performance standards for each step in the process; when it later measured employees' actual results, it found that they were achieving nearly 100 percent compliance with the standards, but turnaround times had grown longer still. How to account for this anomalous result? It turned out that when pressed for time, people conveniently discovered errors on bid requests they were handling, which entitled them to send these back to the preceding department for rework, thereby excluding that request from their measurements.

IBM Credit's experience is not atypical. Organizations often go to great trouble and expense to avoid the radical redesign associated with reengineering. They may reorganize, which means that they don't change work processes at all, only the administrative boxes around the people doing it. Companies downsize, which just means using fewer people to do the same or less work in the same way. Companies try motivational programs, which use incentives to try to get people to work harder.

Existing processes, even if they're the source of a company's business problems, are nonetheless familiar; the organization is comfortable with them. The infrastructure to support them is already in place. Improving them seems so much easier and more "sensible" than throwing them out and starting all over. Incrementalism is the path of least resistance for most organizations. It is also the surest way to fail at reengineering.

• Don't focus on business processes
Not long ago, the progressive management of the U.S. subsidiary of a major European company commissioned several task forces of

workers to address the critical issues of the day: empowerment, teamwork, innovation, customer service, and so on. The task forces' agendas were a lexicon of contemporary business clichés. Each group was given ninety days to develop recommendations as to how the organization could make major progress on its respective issue. The teams received *carte blanche*; no idea would be considered off-limits or too wild. The task forces worked intensively for ninety days and produced precisely nothing. To be sure, they submitted reams of paper full of platitudinous recommendations, but all who read them understood immediately that these meant nothing and that nothing would come of them.

Why did this effort, with so much executive support and widespread participation, end in such failure? Because the problems were poorly defined. "Teamwork" and "empowerment" are abstractions and generalities around which it's impossible to get one's arms. They describe characteristics or attributes that one might want an organization to exhibit, but there is no direct way to achieve them. They are *consequences* of process designs and they can only be achieved in that context. How is one supposed to begin working on empowerment if not through the architecture of the work processes? "Innovation" is also the result of well-designed processes, not a thing in itself. The flaw in this company's efforts, and in similar attempts elsewhere, is that it failed to take a process perspective on the business. Without that, business improvement efforts amount to rearranging deck chairs on the *Titanic*.

• Ignore everything *except* process redesign

A reengineering effort, as we have seen, triggers changes of many kinds. Job designs, organizational structures, management systems—everything associated with the process—must be refashioned in order to maintain a coherent business system diamond.

As we related in Chapter 2, when Ford reengineered its vendor payment process, the effects reached as far as clerks on the receiving dock, who suddenly became decision makers. Instead of just stamping paper with times and dates, they now had to use a computer terminal to determine whether the arriving shipment corresponded to an outstanding order. If not, it was their responsibility to refuse the shipment and send it back. People who formerly had virtually no responsibilities now had to think and make decisions.

At IBM Credit, people who previously knew only how to check credit are now evaluating and pricing entire financing deals. To do this, they not only had to learn new jobs, they had to acquire new attitudes about their jobs.

Capital Holding's Direct Response Group (DRG) rethought its entire approach to the customer and reengineered many processes. As a consequence, DRG had to redesign its job-rating schemes, compensation policies, career paths, recruitment and training programs, promotion policies—practically every management system, in other words—in order to support the new process designs.

Even managers who are anxious for radical process redesign are often frightened by the full range of changes that such redesigns necessitate. We often encounter the following scenario: A senior manager commissions a reengineering team to produce breakthrough improvements for a troublesome process. Some time later the team returns, describes a breakthrough concept, and shows how it will eliminate 90 percent of the cycle time, 95 percent of the cost, and 99 percent of the errors. The manager squirms with joy. The team then proceeds to explain how the redesigned process will require a new job-rating system, the consolidation of numerous departments, the redefinition of management authority, and a different style of labor relations. The senior manager squirms again, but not with joy. "I asked you to reduce costs and errors," he or she says, "not to remake the company." The team then is usually disbanded and its breakthrough concept never heard from again. But remaking the company is precisely what reengineering is about.

• Neglect people's values and beliefs

People need some reason to perform well within the reengineered processes. It isn't enough simply to put new processes in place; managers must motivate employees to rise to the challenge of these processes by supporting the new values and beliefs the processes demand. In other words, management must pay attention to what goes on in people's heads as well as what happens on their desks.

When Ford reengineered the way it paid its vendors, workers' attitudes and behaviors had to shift as well. Purchasing personnel could no longer view vendors as adversaries to be beaten down. They had to be viewed as Ford's partners in a shared business process.

When DRG reengineered its process for reviewing insurance applications, it also had to make a radical change in its culture. Supervisors could no longer be taskmasters, but had to function as providers of service to the employees actually performing the work—making sure that case workers had all the tools and support they needed to do their jobs.

Changes that require shifts in attitude are not easily accepted. Merely giving speeches isn't sufficient. New management systems must cultivate the required values by rewarding behavior that exhibits them. But senior managers must also give speeches about these new values, as well as demonstrate their commitment to them by their personal behavior.

• Be willing to settle for minor results

Big results require big ambitions. A critical test of ambition occurs at that point in a reengineering effort when someone suggests that a modest change will make the process work 10 percent better for practically no cost, in contrast to the pain and suffering engendered by reengineering. The temptation to take the easy path and to settle for the marginal improvement is great. In the long run, however, marginal improvement is no improvement at all, but a detriment.

Marginal improvements, as a rule, further complicate the current process, making it subsequently more difficult to figure out how things really work. Even worse, making additional investments of time or capital into an existing process only discourages management from dumping that process down the road. Most perniciously, taking incremental steps further reinforces a culture of incrementalism, creating a company with no valor or courage.

• Quit too early

It should not be surprising that some companies abandon reengineering or scale back their reengineering goals at the first sign of a problem. They lose their nerve. But we've also seen companies call off their reengineering effort at the first sign of success. As soon as they have something to show for all their pain and suffering they stop. The initial success becomes an excuse to return to the easy life of business as usual. In either case, by failing to persevere the company forgoes the huge payoffs down the road.

• Place prior constraints on the definition of the problem and the scope of the reengineering effort

A reengineering effort is doomed to fail when, before it even begins, corporate management narrowly defines the problem to be solved or limits its scope. Defining the problem and establishing its scope are steps in the reengineering effort itself. Reengineering begins with articulating the objectives that the effort seeks to achieve, not the ways in which these objectives will be met.

The experience of an industrial equipment manufacturer illustrates the point. Senior management told its consultants that the company's order fulfillment process was too expensive. Their charge was to shrink the operating cost of this process.

As the consultants investigated the problem, they talked to the company's customers, all of whom said that they hated practically everything about the company except the equipment it made. If they could buy those same products from someone else, they said, they would do so in a minute.

The higher-ups, insulated from direct contact with their market, thought the problem was the internal cost of order fulfillment, but it really lay in the entire customer service process—fulfillment, support, and communications. Everything in the interface with the customer was broken. Had the consultants accepted their charge at face value and limited themselves to examining the cost of the process, as an internal reengineering team commissioned by management might have been constrained to do under the circumstances, they would not have discovered the real nature of the company's difficulties.

It isn't uncommon for managers at senior levels of large organizations to be so out of touch with customer or production reality that they don't know just how broken some of their business processes are. Insulated from the process level, senior management isn't equipped to define the problem to be solved nor to delimit its scope.

It's also common for companies to state that the target is a business process but then proceed to restrict the reengineering effort to an arbitrary and small segment of the process that happens to fit nearly within existing organizational boundaries. This course is a surefire recipe for failure. Reengineering must break boundaries, not reinforce them. Reengineering must feel disruptive, not comfortable.

Insisting that reengineering be neat is insisting that it not be reengineering.

• Allow existing corporate cultures and management attitudes to prevent reengineering from getting started

A company's prevailing cultural characteristics can inhibit or defeat a reengineering effort before it begins. For instance, if a company operates by consensus, its people will find the top-down nature of reengineering an affront to their sensibilities. Companies whose short-term orientations keep them exclusively focused on quarterly results may find it difficult to extend their vision to reengineering's longer horizons. Organizations with a bias against conflict may be uncomfortable challenging long-established rules. It is executive management's responsibility to anticipate and overcome such barriers.

• Try to make reengineering happen from the bottom up

It is axiomatic that reengineering never, ever happens from the bottom up. There are two reasons why frontline employees and middle managers are unable to initiate and implement a successful reengineering effort, no matter how great the need or how prodigious their talent.

The first reason that the push for reengineering must come from the top of an organization is that people near the front lines lack the broad perspective that reengineering demands. Their expertise is largely confined to the individual functions and departments that they inhabit. They may see very clearly—probably better than anyone else—the narrow problems from which their departments suffer, but it is difficult for them to see a process as a whole and to recognize its poor overall design as the source of their problems. Frontline managers embrace incrementalism more readily than reengineering because they can act incrementally without exceeding the range of their vision.

Second, any business process inevitably crosses organizational boundaries, so no midlevel manager will have sufficient authority to insist that such a process be transformed. Its scope will inevitably transcend his or her domain of responsibility. Furthermore, some of the affected middle managers will correctly fear that dramatic changes to existing processes might diminish their own power, influence, and authority. These managers have much invested in the existing ways of doing things, and the future of the company may be implicitly—and sometimes explicitly—compromised by their own career interests. They fear change because the new rules aren't clear. If radical change threatens to bubble up from below, they may resist it and throttle it. Only strong leadership from above will induce these people to accept the transformations that reengineering brings.

• Assign someone who doesn't understand reengineering to lead the effort
Senior management leadership is a necessary prerequisite for successful reengineering, but not just any senior manager will do. The leader must be someone who is oriented toward operations and

appreciates the relationship between operational performance and financial results. Only a process-oriented senior executive who is capable of thinking about the entire value-added chain—from product concept to sales and service—can lead a reengineering effort. Seniority and authority are not enough; understanding and the right mind-set are critical as well.

• Skimp on the resources devoted to reengineering
The laws of thermodynamics say that you can't get something for nothing. In our context, that means a company cannot achieve the performance breakthroughs that reengineering promises without investing in its reengineering program. The most important component of this investment is the time and attention of the company's best people. Reengineering cannot be entrusted to the semicompetent, the hangers-on with nothing better to do.

Reengineering also demands the direct and personal involvement of senior management. Just as it cannot bubble up from the bottom of the organization, reengineering cannot be delegated down into it. Senior people don't have to do the reengineering themselves. They can deputize helpers and collaborators, but they cannot abdicate the responsibility for the effort to them. Reengineering must be the leader's personal project, with all that it implies. Quarterly progress reviews won't do. The senior management team must invest regular effort in guiding and monitoring the activities of all the reengineering projects underway in the company.

Assigning skimpy resources to the reengineering effort also signals the organization that management doesn't consider the attempt to be terribly important and encourages people to ignore or resist it in the expectation that before long it will have run its course and gone away.

• Bury reengineering in the middle of the corporate agenda
We tell companies that if they don't put reengineering at the top of their agenda, they should leave it off entirely. If management atten-

tion and energy are spread across many different efforts or programs, of which reengineering is only one, reengineering will not get the intense attention that it requires. Without constant management concern, resistance and inertia—the natural tendency of people and organizations to continue doing pretty much what they have always done—will bring the effort to a halt. Only if people recognize that management is committed to reengineering, is concentrating on it, and is giving it regular and close attention, will they reconcile themselves to its inevitability.

• Dissipate energy across a great many reengineering projects
Reengineering requires sharp focus and enormous discipline, which is another way of saying that companies must concentrate their reengineering efforts on a small number of processes at any given time. An organization becomes bewildered rather than energized when it's asked to do too much at once. The customer service, research and development, and sales processes may all need radical redesign, but nothing is likely to happen if a company tries to tackle them all simultaneously unless it has exceptional management capacity. Management's time and attention are limited, and reengineering won't obtain the crucial support it needs if managers have to flit among projects.

• Attempt to reengineer when the CEO is two years from retirement
The CEO or business unit head who is a year or two away from retiring may take a dim and unenthusiastic view of reengineering. This isn't because he or she has grown lazy or no longer cares about the organization's future. Rather, making fundamental changes in business processes will inevitably have major consequences for the structure of the company and many of its management systems. An imminent retiree may simply not want to deal with such complex issues or make commitments that will constrain a successor.

A second problem raised by a CEO close to retirement is the

effect that the impending change at the top is likely to have on other managers. Especially in hierarchical organizations, contenders for a senior post that is about to open up often feel that they are being watched and judged. If so, they may be more interested in individual performance than in being part of a large, collective reengineering effort. Furthermore, they'll have no interest in any program that changes the familiar rules by which they've gained their positions in the organization, and they will want to avoid any possible risk until the succession die is cast.

Beware of CEOs who, near retirement, contend that they are now ready to accept the risks that reengineering entails. "After all," a chief executive may argue, "I have little to lose at this late stage in my career." True, but if they have waited until now to become bold executive managers, they may not, in a short period of time, be able to learn how to behave in the way the rule requires.

• Fail to distinguish reengineering from other business improvement programs

One problem from which many companies—regrettably—don't suffer is a death of business change programs. As times get tougher, purported panaceas proliferate. The business media are brimming over with ideas and programs to make companies better: quality improvement, strategic alignment, "rightsizing," customer-supplier partnerships, innovation, and empowerment, to name a few. Usually these programs are ephemeral. As one corporate wag told us, "Every month, our senior management goes to some seminar and comes home with a new religion. We just hold our breath until they get over it." A danger for reengineering is that employees will see it as just another Program of the Month. This danger will certainly materialize if reengineering is delegated to an impotent staff group. To preclude this possibility, management must make reengineering the responsibility of line managers, not of staff specialists. Moreover, if the company is in fact seriously committed to another business improvement program (such as TQM), then great care must be taken to carefully position reengineering relative to the other program. Otherwise, confusion will result and enormous energy will be expended on pointless internecine warfare about which program is superior.

• Concentrate exclusively on design
Reengineering isn't just about redesign. It's also about translating new designs into reality. The difference between winners and losers at reengineering doesn't usually lie in the quality of their respective ideas, but in what they do with them. With the losers, reengineering never moves beyond the idea phase into implementation.

• Try to make reengineering happen without making anybody unhappy
The aphorism about the need to break eggs to make omelets is very applicable to reengineering. It would be nice to say that reengineering is a win-win program that leaves everyone better off; it would be nice, but it would also be a lie. Reengineering isn't to everyone's advantage. Some employees do have a vested interest in current operations, some people will lose their jobs, and some workers may be uncomfortable with their jobs postreengineering. Trying to please everyone is a hopeless ambition that will either devalue reengineering to a program of incremental change or delay its implementation into the future.

• Pull back when people resist making reengineering's changes
That people resist change shouldn't surprise anyone, especially not those in charge of a company's reengineering effort. Resistance is an inevitable reaction to major change. The first step in managing resistance, however, is to expect it and not let it set the effort back.

We have heard some managers say that reengineering failed in their companies because people resisted change. This is like saying that Newton's second law—a body in motion tends to stay in motion—is a major cause of automobile accidents. It isn't Newton's law but people's failure to heed it that causes crashes, and management's failure to anticipate and plan for the inevitable resistance that reengineering will encounter is the true cause of its failure.

• Drag the effort out

Reengineering is stressful for everyone in a company, and stretching it over a long time period extends the discomfort. Our experience suggests that twelve months should be long enough for a company to move from articulation of a case for action to the first field release of a reengineered process. Take longer, and people will become impatient, confused, and distracted. They will conclude that reengineering is another bogus program and the effort will fall apart.

Undoubtedly, there are more paths that lead to reengineering failure than those we have just listed. People are remarkably resourceful in finding new ways to drop the ball. However, one strong thread runs through all the pitfalls that we have encountered. That thread is the role of senior management. If reengineering fails, no matter what the proximate cause, the underlying reason can invariably be traced to senior managers' inadequate understanding or lendership of the reengineering effort. Reengineering is always born in the executive suite. All too often, it dies there as well.

Despite the opportunities for failure, we are heartened by the many successes of reengineering. Organizations that approach reengineering with understanding, commitment, and strong executive leadership *will* succeed at it. The payoffs of successful reengineering are spectacular—for the individual company, for its managers and its employees, and for the American economy as a whole. The time for hesitation is gone; the time for action is now.

EPILOGUE

Despite their well-publicized difficulties, American businesses are not yet an endangered species. Those that we cite throughout this book are themselves proof that American companies can change to compete in the evolving world economy. They have learned that an enviable reputation, good financial controls, and a debt-free balance sheet no longer guarantee survival. Surviving in today's world demands strong executive leadership, an intense focus on customers and their needs, and superior process design and execution. Reengineering is one of the tools companies must possess and know how to use to acquire those prerequisites to success.

In the last decade, many miracle cures have been prescribed for the ills of American business. Most of them have passed through the patients without discernible effect.

Reengineering, in contrast, promises no miracle cure. It offers no quick, simple, and painless fix. On the contrary, it entails difficult, strenuous work. It requires that people running companies and working in them change how they think as well as what they do. It requires that companies replace their old practices with entirely new ones. Doing so isn't easy. It cannot be accomplished with motivational lectures and catchy wall posters.

Although we have explored reengineering at some length, we have barely scratched the surface of the topic, as readers who attempt reengineering in their own companies will discover. For instance, we have written only a little about how organizations can actually make reengineering happen. A methodology for conducting a reengineering effort, the orchestration of the change campaign, the design and timing of releases of newly redesigned processes, and tactics for dealing with the most common problems that arise in implementation are issues that go beyond the scope of a single book.

Moreover, other important questions about reengineering as yet have no conclusive answers. For example, "What impact will the reengineering of American companies have on the U.S. economy?" And how will reengineering's flattening of corporate hierarchies affect managers and executives accustomed to gauging their self-worth by their positions within an organization?

The uncertainties of reengineering, however, cannot be used as an excuse to put off what must be done. Leading corporations in nearly every industry have already begun to reengineer. As more companies bring their key processes up to higher levels of performance, the reengineering option becomes a competitive necessity for others in the same industry. Reengineering by even one key participant in a market creates a new benchmark level that all competitors must meet.

Reengineering is still a new endeavor; all of us engaged in it are pioneers. The world of the industrial revolution is giving way to an era of a global economy, powerful information technologies, and relentless change. The curtain is rising on the age of reengineering. Those who respond to its challenges will write the new rules of American business. All that is needed is the will to succeed and the courage to begin.

Frequently Asked Questions (FAQs)

The chance to add a chapter to a published book creates several opportunities. We've decided to avail ourselves of two of them.

The first is the opportunity to clarify and amplify certain points that we tried to make in the original book but that apparently didn't come through as clearly as we had hoped. Several of these gaps have prompted readers to pepper us with questions. We'll use this new chapter to answer them and hope that the answers clarify our original thinking.

Second, there is the opportunity to update the book in some areas, to incorporate in it some things that we've learned since it was published. Therefore, we will use this chapter to answer some of the most frequently asked questions we've received from readers. We assume that if a lot of people bothered to ask a question, a lot more would be interested in the answer. In addition, we'll answer some questions that haven't often been asked but should have been: questions that give us an excuse to amplify the book in an important way.

The question most often put to us concerns our statement in the book that some 50 to 70 percent of reengineering attempts fail to deliver the intended dramatic results. Many people have wondered if it isn't foolhardy to undertake a program with such a high failure rate.

In reporting that failure rate, we were being historical, not predictive. We say that more than 50 percent of reengineering efforts *have* failed, not that they inevitably *will* fail. Reengineering programs fail because the people undertaking them make common, avoidable mistakes, which we list and discuss in Chapter 13, "Succeeding at Reengineering." However, if you avoid these mistakes, which is very possible, your chances of success at reengineering are good. Indeed, a company with a well-planned, well-executed reengineering program will almost always succeed. Also, failure doesn't mean that reengineering stops forever—it usually stalls and then restarts as the company gets itself refocused and remobilized. It cannot stop—the business imperative is too great. As we have said, reengineering is not like roulette. It's like chess, where you win if you play well. Read Chapter 13 again. Avoiding those mistakes almost guarantees success at reengineering.

- Isn't reengineering just another in a long line of management fads that attract a lot of short-term attention but have little impact over the long term? If not, why not?

No, it's not a fad, but thanks for asking.

First, let's define the word. Lots of so-called management fads were originally good ideas that were either oversold or used in ways they were never intended. Consider quality circles or management by walking around. Were these fads? No, they were sound ideas that, in the case of quality circles, were never well understood in context and, in the case of MBWA, were burdened with unrealistic expectations. Take quality circles out of a TQM context, and they're a waste of time. If you count on MBWA to bring your overhead costs down, it will disappoint you. There are no miracle cures in management, but managers have a bad habit of buying potions that lay claim to miracles.

There are two reasons why reengineering is not a fad. First, it is not a miracle drug; it is hard work. Reengineering does not offer a single, narrow technique to solve all problems; rather, it is a massive undertaking that entails rethinking every aspect of the business. Reengineering will take about a decade to run its course through the first group of businesses to embrace the concept and embark on the process. The companies we have written about are in that vanguard. No mere fad takes a decade to work out.

Second, reengineering is not a fad because it works. Properly applied, it delivers what it promises. In fact, companies around the world have achieved unprecedented performance improvements by following its principles.

• What is the difference between reengineering and TQM?
Reengineering and TQM are neither identical nor in conflict; they are complementary. While they share a focus on customers and processes, there are also important differences between them. Reengineering gets a company where it needs to be fast; TQM moves a company in the same direction, but more slowly. Reengineering is about dramatic, radical change; TQM involves incremental adjustment. Both have their place. TQM should be used to keep a company's processes tuned up between the periodic process replacements that only reengineering can accomplish.

In addition, TQM, once it is built into a company's culture, can go on working without much day-to-day attention from management. Reengineering, in contrast, is an intensive, top-down, vision-driven effort that requires nonstop senior management participation and support.

• Has your understanding of reengineering changed since the book was written?
It has. We originally defined reengineering as "the fundamental rethinking and radical redesign of business processes to achieve dramatic improvements in critical, contemporary measures of performance . . . ," and we said there were four key words in that definition: "fundamental," "radical," "dramatic," and "processes." Of the four, we originally thought "radical" was the most important. Since we wrote that, our emphasis has changed. We now think that the most important concept to grasp is "process."

We've changed our minds because even more fundamental in reengineering than the idea of doing things differently is making one's processes the heart of one's organization. The essence of our approach is to manage businesses around their processes. Sometimes they will require radical redesign, and sometimes they will not.

This shift of emphasis is not a wholesale change in our thinking, but a refinement of our understanding of what is most crucial to reengineering.

• Did you invent reengineering?

Absolutely not. At most, we discovered it, which is altogether different. Companies were doing reengineering before we came along, but in a haphazard fashion and without a real understanding of what it was about. We have sought to define, clarify, and systematize reengineering so that it would be a more deliberate process. Similarly, Peter Drucker was once asked if he had "invented" management, which was obviously something that people had been doing for years. Drucker replied that his book *The Practice of Management* made it possible for people to learn how to manage, something that up to then, he said, only a few geniuses seemed able to do, and which nobody could replicate. "I sat down and made a discipline of it. . . . Look," Drucker added, "if you can't replicate something because you don't understand it, then it really hasn't been invented; it's only been done."

• What kinds of companies are reengineering and what kinds are not?

The distribution of companies actively reengineering across industry lines is not uniform, so generalization is difficult. However, companies in particular industries do tend to cluster within one of three broad categories: companies relatively far along in the reengineering process, those getting started, and those hanging back.

Insurance companies probably do more reengineering than companies in any other industry. Other industries heavily represented in the advanced group include telecommunications and electric power utilities. Among the industries that have come more recently to reengineering are chemicals, electronics, computers, pharmaceuticals, and consumer goods. Retailers, banks, and government agencies are generally still lagging.

Why should insurance companies have jumped so far ahead of banks in reengineering, since both are financial service businesses? Maybe it's a function of their contrasting leadership styles. Bank executives are often former loan officers or traders—dealmakers, in other words. In their experience, success comes from having the right person with the right information make the right decision. The idea of process as key is somewhat foreign to their thinking. In the insurance industry, on the other hand, almost everybody at the top has a background in operations and is therefore more comfortable with the idea of process and the pursuit of operational excellence.

• Does reengineering apply to government and other public-sector institutions?
Without a doubt. As we say early in the book, reengineering is about rethinking the organization of work. Therefore, it applies to any organization in which work is performed.

In fact, the National Performance Review, chaired by Vice President Al Gore in the summer of 1993, led to the Reinventing Government (ReGo) initiative, which extensively embraces the reengineering principles articulated here. However, reengineering governmental organizations poses some special problems.

One unique challenge facing reengineering in the public sector is the difficulty of measuring performance. Private-sector organizations can use profit as a yardstick of success, and profit is linked to a number of different variables. It can be improved by lowering costs, for instance, or by increasing quality and service and therefore driving up revenues. The bottom line represents a simple way of telling whether the business is improving or not. Most public-sector institutions, however, have only a cost line, which makes it hard to assess tradeoffs between improving services and reducing costs.

Not surprisingly, many of the government agencies at the forefront of reengineering are tax departments and departments like the Veterans Administration. Tax departments can clearly measure the cost of operations versus revenues raised, and the VA may soon have to compete in the private sector with other health-care providers.

A second difficulty is that breaking down departmental barriers within a corporation is much easier than breaking them down between government agencies. The federal government, in particular, is not a single enterprise but rather a network of enterprises. Reengineering is most easily performed at the agency level (e.g., the IRS or Social Security Administration), yet government work frequently crosses agency lines. For example, people entering the United States from abroad may have to stand in three separate lines: one for Immigration and Naturalization, one for the Customs Service, and another established by the USDA for agricultural inspection. The traveler has to suffer with the redundant processes that result from agency jurisdictions. One agency might reengineer its processes to perfection, but the traveler would still face three lines, even if one of them were now shorter.

Another reason that government is one of the notable laggards in reengineering, politics aside, is that reengineering is about achieving operational excellence, and most government agency heads have very little experience with operations. They are primarily policy people; reengineering is often a real stretch for them.

• Does a company need to be large to reengineer?
No. This is another area in which our thinking has shifted a bit since we wrote the book. Our early reengineering experiences took place in large, multibillion-dollar organizations, but now we

see that most of the real reengineering in these organizations occurred within smaller, constituent units such as divisions. We've also recently seen reengineering successfully deployed in quite small businesses. So we've become convinced that any organization that's too large to get everyone around the same table is large enough for reengineering, because such an organization will develop the problems that reengineering addresses. Does everybody in the organization know everybody else? Can everyone perform everyone else's job? If not, then the organization is subject to the kinds of compartmentalization and fragmentation that reengineering roots out.

Too many small companies look and operate like large ones. They may be smaller, but they've already adopted the old conventional ways, and their processes are as hopelessly fragmented as those of their larger cousins. They clearly need reengineering. This need is reinforced by the fact that their large competitors are likely to be reengineering and bringing up their performance standards. No longer are small companies necessarily more nimble than their larger competitors just because they're small.

Even if a small company doesn't immediately need to reengineer itself, an understanding of the principles and procedures of reengineering can be very valuable. First, it can make the company into a better vendor, customer, or partner for large corporations that have reengineered—they know the terrain. Second, small companies that are still lean can use this experience against the encroaching flab of bureaucracy. An ounce of prevention . . .

The principles of reengineering can even be applied in start-up companies and other new ventures. Although it may be awkward to call the process "reengineering" when there is nothing in place to *re*engineer, the same principles for organizing work apply to new firms as to established companies. A good example of this is Astra-Merck, a new joint venture of two major pharmaceutical companies that organized itself from the outset around the principles laid down in this book.

• Is reengineering purely an American phenomenon?

Absolutely not. Although American companies have been in the vanguard of this movement, reengineering has quickly spread around the world. This book has been a bestseller from Korea to Brazil. While the concept fits the U.S. penchant for innovation, change, and focusing on tomorrow rather than yesterday, other countries—particularly in Latin America and East Asia—are finding it highly appealing as well. Not all countries take so naturally to reengineering, however.

• Can reengineering succeed in a unionized environment?

Yes. It's not organized labor that most often tries to block or scuttle a company's reengineering efforts, but its middle managers, whose power and turf are likely to be diminished. However, reengineering can raise hackles among union members, especially when a company has a history of bad labor relations or when previous downsizing or head-count reductions have sharpened people's job security concerns.

While some employees may lose their jobs as a result of a corporate reengineering program, reengineering is itself a process for reorganizing work, not eliminating workers. So the best precaution against worker opposition to reengineering is to get people engaged in the process as early as possible. Unionized companies that have successfully reengineered have typically involved the union leadership in the reengineering process from the outset.

When union resistance develops, however, a strategy of firm commitment is a company's only choice while it continues to keep employees—unionized or not—engaged in the process. Union leadership that understands reengineering and why it is being done is unlikely to push its unhappiness with reengineering as far as a strike.

• Do I start with one process? Two processes? Everything?

It's a question not of how many processes but of which ones. You can undertake to reengineer a great many ancillary processes and achieve hardly any effect on the corporate bottom line. Or you can select one or two of the core processes that are critical to your business objectives and make a huge difference.

It's just as hard to reengineer the little processes as the big ones, because any reengineering program is going to cross departmental boundaries and functional lines and create unrest. You might as well make the chaos worth your time and effort and start with the processes that will yield the biggest payoffs.

• Wouldn't the need to reengineer disappear for most companies if the economy improved?

The need would not, but the will might. A recession or a lagging recovery intensifies the pressures on companies to fix what ails them, and just because this pressure eases during an economic upturn doesn't mean that processes are any less in need of attention. When the tough times return—and they always do—the problems will recur and the delay will have made reengineering even more difficult to accomplish.

• A company reengineers. Then what?

In the aftermath of reengineering, the newly reengineered processes have to be managed to achieve the performance levels of which they are capable; however, process management is a new challenge for most companies.

Reengineering creates an organizational environment in which hierarchy is diminished, workers are more skilled, and structures are more flexible. The emphasis in this environment is on work, not on administration. Learning how to work and to manage in such an organization is a critical requirement for harvesting the benefits of reengineering.

Before long, however, the time will come for the next round of process redesign and reengineering. Companies that got fifty years of use out of their last set of process blueprints may not get more than five to ten years out of the next set. Change has become a permanent fixture of our business lives, and with it comes a need for recurrent reengineering.

We suspect that the next round of reengineering won't be as traumatic as the first one. A company that reengineers and thereby reconstitutes fragmented work, eliminates functional rivalries, and flattens its organizational hierarchy probably won't find it as difficult to undertake another reengineering effort. Our long-term goal must be to institutionalize a capacity for reengineering in our companies so that they view change as the norm rather than as an aberration. Creating such a company is, however, not a minor endeavor; it is, indeed, a topic for another book.

INDEX